Linen Threads and Broom Twines

An Irish and American Album and Directory of the People of the Dunbarton Mill

Greenwich, New York
1879-1952

Volume 1
The Album

William T. Ruddock

HERITAGE BOOKS
2006

HERITAGE BOOKS

AN IMPRINT OF HERITAGE BOOKS, INC.

Books, CDs, and more—Worldwide

For our listing of thousands of titles see our website
at
www.HeritageBooks.com

Published 2006 by
HERITAGE BOOKS, INC.
Publishing Division
65 East Main Street
Westminster, Maryland 21157-5026

Other books by the author:

*Linen Threads and Broom Twines: An Irish and American Album
and Directory of the People of the Dunbarton Mill,
Greenwich, New York, 1879-1952, Volume 2: The Directory*

International Standard Book Number: 978-0-7884-0770-8

Table of Contents - Volume 1

Acknowledgments

The Banbridge District and Historical Society	For their work on the local history of the Banbridge, Ireland district including Gilford. They have been very helpful in connecting me with resources in Ireland.
Blue Mountain Industries	Who provided much help in the history of the Linen Thread Co. Special thanks to Harry E. Flanders.
Borderbund Banner Blue Division	For approval to use the Social Security Death index information from Automated Archives, Inc. 1991.
Grafton Historical Society, Inc.	For the information they provided concerning the history of the Finlayson-Bousfield mill in North Grafton, Massachusetts. Special thanks to Bob Wilson.
The Greenwich Journal	For the men and women, who through dedication and hard work, have put out a superior weekly paper. This book would not have been possible without this valuable resource. Special thanks Sally Tefft for her support and authorization to quote from the paper.
Alan Harris	For his help in editing this work.
George Herrmann, Inc.	Who provided samples of flax yarn, scutched flax and flax noils. Special thanks to Rosemary Hamway.
Sara Idleman	For her help in reviewing a draft version of this book and her work in interviewing Irish linen workers. Particular thanks for her recording the oral histories of Ivy Cooke Brown Cahill and Jane Feenan Connor
Isaac Jackson	For his story found on page 144. Also for his help in obtaining pictures of the Dunbarton, and for his interest and support of this project.
The Lansing Public Library	For supporting my endless interlibrary loan requests for copies of the Greenwich Journal. Special thanks to Mrs. Stevens.
LDS Family History Library	For their work of preserving worldwide records including state census, Irish vital records and family history. Special thanks to the East Lansing Branch and Sister Benjamin.

The Library of Michigan	For maintaining such an outstanding library with such a wide variety of materials. Everything from US government records, census returns, business directories and various publications were valuable sources for this book.
Dr. Alec Lyons	For his help in tracking down pictures and information about the Dunbar McMaster & Co. in Gilford Ireland.
Betty Messenger	For her fabulous work Picking Up the Linen Threads, and for her encouragement to this project.
New York State Library	It was through their foresight that the Greenwich Journal and the People's Journal were microfilmed. It was through their lending policies that I was able to research these valuable documents while living in the Lansing area.
Renfrew Public Library	For their help in researching the Finlayson-Bousfield Company of Johnstone, Scotland.
Sanborn Map Company	Sanborn Insurance Maps & Sanborn Map Information, Provided courtesy of "The Sanborn Map Company" a division of EDR Sanborn, Inc. Copyright 1996, The Sanborn Map Company, 629 Fifth Avenue, Pelham, NY 10803, Tel (914) 738-1649
Dianna Till	For her help in editing this work.
Jane Whitaker	She provided much valuable information on the mill Strike. She was a constant help throughout the entire project.

Thanks also for pictures from the following:

Wilson V. Binger, Carol Hand, Jane Whitaker, Christie Lyttle, Florence Amos, Sonny Nolan, Hazel Carp, Arthur Wilcox, Jean (Bright) LeClaire

Most special thanks must go to my family, Eldonna, Thomas and David. They have been very supportive of this project and provided help beyond measure.

Introduction

"A Brighter Day for Greenwich" was the title of the People's Journal article of October 9, 1879. This article predicted great prosperity as it announced the establishment of what would become the Dunbarton mill in Greenwich. There are few predictions of the future which turn out as close to reality as this one! This mill operated almost continuously for 72 years of bright days for Greenwich. Although the Dunbarton stopped producing linen thread over 40 years ago the mark of the mill can still be seen today.

The village of Greenwich itself lies along the Batten Kill river and is situated in the hills which separate the Adirondack Mountains of New York and the Green Mountains of Vermont. The village was settled by people from Rhode Island, Connecticut and Massachusetts in the late 1700s. In 1809 the village incorporated as Union Village. By the mid 1800s the village changed its name to Greenwich and is proudly pronounced green witch.

The establishment of the Dunbarton greatly changed this village of New England origins. It did this primarily by bringing to Greenwich a special class of people. These people dedicated their productive lives to the Dunbarton mill. They took flax, a natural fiber, from its raw form and converted it into finished thread. This thread was so strong that a loop of it could not be broken by even the strongest man. They were well trained and hard working. They were a loyal workforce, laboring for up to sixty years with the Dunbarton mill. Most came from Ireland to bring their expertise to the mill. They grew old to see their children and grand-children make a living by working in the Dunbarton. This book seeks to explore, document, and honor the lives and efforts of these hardworking people.

Even though the Dunbarton stopped producing thread five years before I was born, the mark of the people of the Dunbarton was indelibly written on the neighborhood in Greenwich, New York in which I grew up. In fact, the homes on lower Bleeker Street, lower Hill street, VanNess Ave, Washington, and John Streets were built to house those who worked in this mill. Nearly every family who lived in these homes could trace their ancestry to one or more who came from Ireland to work in the Dunbarton. Even the corner store which was then run by Lathrop Chase, was first established by William Wilson, a Dunbarton foreman turned businessman.

Both of my parent's families were directly influenced by the Dunbarton mill. My great-grandfather George Ruddock was born in Gilford, Ireland. He worked for the Dunbar, McMaster & Co. in Gilford and in 1893 he came to this country, settling first at Amsterdam, New York with relatives there. A short time later he came to Greenwich to work in the Dunbarton mill. He was a flax hackler and later was a foreman in the mill. He met Sarah Redpath, also an Irish immigrant who worked in the mill, and married her in 1901. George and Sarah lived a modest life in Greenwich, where they purchased their first home on Washington Street and later bought a larger home on Bleeker Street. It was in this Bleeker Street home that I grew up. My father and sister still own and reside in this home.

James Bright, who came from Gilford in 1880 as clerk in the Dunbarton office, became the mill's superintendent and eventually the mill's manager. His son, John Bright, was a mill manager for the Stevens & Thompson company in Middle Falls, New York. Middle Falls is a hamlet in the Town of Greenwich. John Bright purchased a farm in Middle Falls on the condition that my maternal Grandfather, Frank Humphrey, would run the farm operations. John was to act as mentor for my Grandfather. He was directly responsible for establishing my Grandfather as a successful farmer, and made it possible for him to purchase this farm on very fair terms.

The Dunbarton brought people who influenced the very heart of Greenwich. During its early years, the Dunbarton brought hundreds of Irish immigrants to work here. The Dunbarton work force also brought with them their own spirit and desire to make for themselves a better way of life than they thought was possible in their native country. It is this spirit and desire that has been implanted in all who are descended from this group. They passed on the idea that hard work and a stick to it attitude will, in the end, bare fruit.

Days were bright in Greenwich because of the steady employment created by the Dunbarton. This mill provided great prosperity to the village. Even during the great depression, the Dunbarton increased to two shifts instead of staying on a single shift. This steady employment led to a stable economy for Greenwich.

The People of the Dunbarton

Just say the word Dunbarton to any old timer in Greenwich and you will more than likely get a smile. Why should mentioning the name of this mill get this almost universal reaction?

The answer is simple. It is the Dunbarton workforce that make folks who can remember smile. Those who worked in the Dunbarton were a special class. They were mostly Irish with Irish ways. They spoke with an Irish brogue and ate potatoes at every meal. They were often called "the old Irish". They were both Catholic and Protestant. They were hardworking and serious by nature. The spent their lives in community with each other and with the larger community of the village of Greenwich.

Here are just a few examples from the Dunbarton's large workforce:

♦   George Jackson who would leave a dime for a cola for the spinners after he had fixed one of the frames;
♦   Bill Burns who said that he was told in the old country that his job was good for life when he was asked to retire;

- Joseph Lyttle who sold goods from door to door after working 10 hours in the mill;
- Jimmy Ryan who was also deputy sheriff in addition to his duties at the mill;
- Billy Reid who was a barber in addition to his duties as elevator man of the Dunbarton;
- Thomas Doubleday who showed the town how to dance at a rally;
- Thomas Wilson who, when told that the big house on Washington Square was beyond his means, got just mad enough to buy it anyway;
- Joseph Henderson who told the Presbyterian minister just what he thought right during the preaching of the word;
- Mary J. McAllister who sat high in her seat at the preparer's table and showed the younger women what to do;
- George "Doc" Daisy who liked the office windows opened and brought his dog to work each and every day;
- Belzora Bolich who read taro cards and tea leaves;
- Rose (Nolan) Murphy who told the people of Greenwich in no uncertain terms why a pay cut was not acceptable to her and her fellow strikers;
- William John Wilson who built his own foot bridge across the Batten Kill in order to shorten his walk to work each day; and
- Ida Flansburgh who went each week to the bank with her bag and brought the weekly payroll to the mill.

These are just a few of the large cast of characters who formed the fabric of the Dunbarton community. Through the bonds of work and living together, the mill community dealt with all the complexities of life. They saw children born, the daily struggle to raise a family, the constant need to keep the family finances afloat, the death (sometimes tragic death) of friends and loved ones, the need for housing, heat, and clothing. This community was quite unique from other New England mill town communities in that it was quite specialized. The manufacturing of linen thread was not something just anyone could do. It took great skill and knowledge to pull off. This community was also unique in its relationship to its sister communities of Paterson, New Jersey and Gilford, Ireland where linen thread was also produced and where many Irish folks lived.

The people of the Dunbarton are likeable in their own right. Remembering them cannot help but bring a smile. This book attempts to look at them. Not just as a class of people but individually as well. This book will name names and tell as much as can be said about these special people. It is hoped that the reader will enjoy them as much as the compiler has enjoyed learning about them.

Notes on Reading of This Book

I have used the word Irish throughout this book to mean the people who came from Ireland to work in the mill. Strictly speaking, the Protestant immigrants would have called themselves Scots-Irish or Orange Irish while the Catholic immigrants would have been referred to as Irish. While these distinctions were very important among the groups, I have generalized their relationships so that both are included in the group I call Irish. I apologize for the confusion that this may cause.

To my knowledge no master list exists of those who worked in the Dunbarton. Thus, this book was created by reviewing every source that I could get access to. I began this work as an outgrowth of my own interest in family history. As such, I was most interested in recording in one place the individual stories of those who worked in the mill. It is the individual histories twisted and spun together that produce the strong thread of history presented here.

I apologize for any and all names that I have unknowingly left out of this history.

I also need to indicate that I have used the references The Greenwich Journal, The Journal, and The People's Journal interchangeably. The weekly paper in Greenwich actually has held several names during the times that have been quoted:

Title	Publication dates
The People's Journal	before 1879 through Vol. 55 No. 15 (April 1, 1896)
The Greenwich Journal	Vol. 55 No. 16 (April 8, 1896) through Vol. 82 No. 26 (June 25, 1924)
The Greenwich Journal and Fort Edward Advertiser	Vol. 26 No. 27 (July 2, 1924) through Vol. 128 No. 10 (Nov 2, 1969)

Today the paper is know as The Journal-Press which is a contraction of The Greenwich Journal and Salem Press.

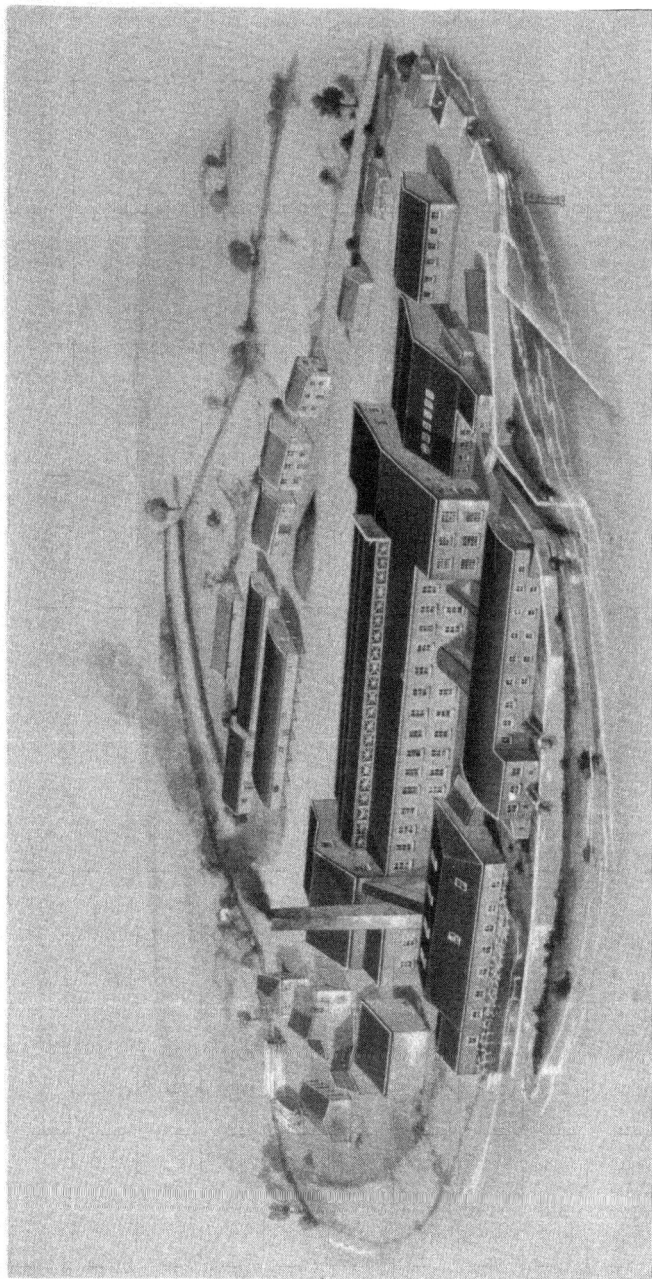

Architect's drawing of the Dunbarton mill of Greenwich, New York circa 1920, Whackle co. Drawing now in possession of the Greenwich Historical Society and hung for many years in the home of the Wm George Jackson family.

Broom Twine and Shoe Thread made at the Dunbarton Mill. Spools in possession of Ike Jackson.

Chapter I Flax and the Production of Linen

In this chapter we will explore the production of linen thread and how it was made. It is hoped this background information will assist in understanding just what was made, how it was made and who made it at the Dunbarton.

A Little on Linen

Linen is thread or fabric made from flax fiber. Flax fiber is one of the oldest materials to be used by humans for the production of man-made cloth. Linen has been found with the Swiss Lake dwellers. Linen cloth has been found in ancient cultures in Egypt and Mesopotamia. For over 5000 years Flax has been cultivated in Egypt. The ancient Egyptians were able to work flax with only hand implements to such a high state of fineness that examples of linen fabric have been found which have more than 500 threads per inch.

During the middle ages virtually every fabric was made from linen - this is the reason that the word linen can be used to mean everything from tablecloths to underwear and from sheets to wall paper. Linen fabrics have many very fine qualities including strength, luster, durability, and coolness. Linen absorbs water very well.

Growing Flax and Processing the Fiber

Flax is only one of the many fibers which come from vegetables. Ramie, hemp and jute also are fibers which come from the stalks of plants. Abaca and henquen fibers come from the leaves of plants. Seed fiber is the basis of cotton.

The flax plant (Linum Usitatissimum) is of the order Linaceae. Flax grows as a long and narrow stalk. From this main stalk grows alternately light green leaves. The stems are crowned with light blue flowers. From these flowers develop small reddish-brown capsules the size of peas which hold the seeds of the plant. The seeds are small and shiny and can be used to make linseed oil.

The stalk of flax, which grows from eighteen to thirty inches, consists of a woody core, a layer of flax fiber, and the outer bark. The layer of flax fiber consists of bundles of long fibers which run in symmetrical layers from the roots to the flowers. These bundles of fiber are held together by a gum-like substance.

At the time the Dunbarton began operations, the process of growing flax was very complicated. It was also very labor intensive. Although many improvements have been made in the culture of flax, it remains a very specialized crop indeed. During the time that the Dunbarton was in operation flax was grown for three primary uses:

1)   Production of fiber for thread and cloth. When flax was grown for this reason it was harvested before the seeds were fully ripe. This prevents combining this use with production of seeds.

2)   Production of seeds (linseed). Linseed was of great commercial value for its oil. Linseed oil when dry creates a waterproof shell. This property made it very useful as a base for paint. The remains of the crushed seed make very good food for cattle. Linseed oil was also combined with flax fiber and dried to produce linoleum. Linoleum was a floor covering widely used in homes.

3)   Production of fiber for use in paper.

The following process was used to cultivate flax and prepare it for processing in a thread mill:

1)   The land was first prepared by plowing, manuring and leveling. The seed was sown in rows 8 - 10 feet apart. The seed was sown by hand using about two to four bushels of seed per acre. By sowing the seeds close together the plant grows tall and narrow with few branches. Once sown the field was then harrowed with a hand harrow and rolled.

2)   When the flax had grown to a height of about 3 inches it was weeded thoroughly. This process was done by women and children crawling on their hands and knees to pull the weeds. They worked toward the wind so that the plants would be gently lifted back upright once weeding was done.

3)   The flax was grown to the desired age. The best indicator of when it was time to harvest the flax was the seed which turned from green to brown. Flax was harvested at the right moment during this time when the seeds change color. For the production of fine thread the flax was harvested earlier.

4)   Harvesting was done by pulling the entire flax plant from the earth. Flax was never cut. To do so would mean injuring the fibers which extended into the root system. To pull the flax a handful was grabbed near the seed pods of the plant and it was pulled from the ground with a jerk. The dirt was then kicked from the roots.

5)   Once pulled, the flax was gathered into sheaves and stacked to dry.

6)   The leaves, seed capsules, and flowers were removed from the flax by passing the flax through a set of combs designed to catch these parts of the plant. This process was called rippling.

7)   The next step was to ret the flax. The purpose of this process to ret the outer "bark" of the flax plant. The retting process was actually a process

of fermentation which acts on the gum which binds the fibers. The fermentation was driven by bacteria which were already present on the plant. All that needed to be done was to provide the right conditions to get the bacteria working. There were three alternative approaches that were used in the process of retting:

a) The flax was placed in crates which were then submerged in a flowing stream. This was a process called cold water retting and was used in Belgium.

b) The flax was placed in pools of stagnant water near a stream. As fermentation progressed, the stalks of flax became coated in air bubbles as a natural by product of fermentation. For this reason the flax was weighted down with stones to keep it under the water. Once retted, the flax was be lifted from the water without use of tools so as to keep from damaging the fibers. This method was adopted in Ireland.

c) Dew retting was used in the United States and Canada. The flax was allowed to lay in the field after it was pulled where the moisture from dew allows fermentation to occur.

Regardless of the process chosen, the flax was ready for the next step when about 50% of the gum had been removed. The central woody core should have been somewhat soft but still intact. It should have been easy to separate the fibers from the core of the plant.

After retting the flax was laid out to dry. Once dry it was placed in bundles for storage. At this point the flax is known as flax straw.

8) The woody core of the straw must then be broken. This was done either by a breaking machine which passed the flax straw through a series of rollers or the straw was beaten with wooden mallets.

9) After the woody core had been broken the flax was then scutched. There were two ways to scutch flax:

a) The flax plants were beaten with a scutching knife to remove the outer "bark" of the flax plant. During scutching the woody core was also removed. A scutching knife was a blunt wooden knife about 12 inches long with a handle on the end.

b) This process was also done in a flax or scutching mill. A scutching mill utilizes a series of blades which spin on a vertical axis. The flax was then placed at right angles into the spinning blades. This process leaves the flax free of most of its outer bark and its woody core is removed.

At the time that the Dunbarton mill was first opened, there were four mills in Greenwich that were in the business of producing scutched flax from the flax that was grown locally (see "Flax in Washington and Rensselaer Counties" on page 23).

Making Linen Thread From Scutched Flax

Early in the Dunbarton's history, the process of making linen thread began with scutched flax. In this case both roughing and hackling operations were carried on at the Dunbarton. Shortly after WWI the Dunbarton began receiving hackled flax. The basic steps necessary to make thread from scutched flax were as follows:

1) Roughing. The scutched flax was first roughed. Roughing was done at first by hand by passing the scutched flax through a wide comb with wide teeth. Hand roughing was later replaced by machine. This process straightened out the flax fibers and prepared them for the process of hackling.

2) Hackling. The next step in the process was the process of hackling the flax. This was entirely a hand process until late in the Dunbarton's history. Flax fiber was hackled by passing the flax fibers through a comb called a hackle. The purpose of this step was to remove any remaining outer bark from the inner flax fiber, and to remove any remaining gum between the fibers. The material removed was called "tow". At this point in the process we now have what was called "dressed line" or "dressed flax". Dressed line looks much like a bundle of horse's tail hair (for more information see "Flax Dressers or Hacklers" on page 7, 22).

3) Sorting. The hackled flax was then sorted into lots of similar length and quality. The longer, finer lots were destined for fine thread while the shorter were used to make coarser thread.

4) Spreading. This was a specialized form of a "drawing" process (see next step). Flax fiber was placed on a spreading table and fed into several sets of gill drawing rollers. As many as eight sets of rollers may be fed at a single spreading table. The flax was fed in overlapping bundles. The eight or so lines of fiber were re-combined to form a single sliver of fiber and the sliver was deposited in a canister. A sliver of flax was a loose ribbon-like arrangement of fiber.

Principles of Drawing

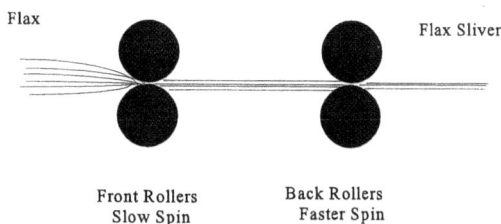

Flax   Flax Sliver

Front Rollers   Back Rollers
Slow Spin   Faster Spin

Principles of Doubling

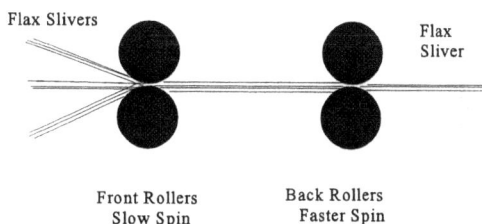

Flax Slivers   Flax
                                                                Sliver

Front Rollers   Back Rollers
Slow Spin   Faster Spin

5)   Drawing and Doubling. When flax was spun at a spinning wheel, the flax
      fibers were "drawn" into the flyer and spindle at a pace and thickness
      determined by how the spinner lets the fiber pass through his or her fingers.
      This process was accomplished mechanically using pairs of rollers. The
      flax fiber passed through one pair of rollers and then passed through a
      second pair. The second pair traveled at a faster speed. In this way the
      flax fiber was thinned out or drawn out into what was known as a sliver.
      Between the two sets of rollers were a set of fine combs that move with the
      fiber. These combs were called gills and prevent the shorter fibers from
      drawing too easily which would make the resulting sliver uneven.

      The sliver of fiber from the Spreading operation was then passed through
      a series of drawing operations. At each step the sliver becomes finer and
      finer. Often the drawn slivers would then be re-combined in a process
      called doubling. Doubling of slivers helped insure consistency in the
      weight of sliver per unit of length. Consistent slivers meant consistent
      thread which equated to quality. The drawing and doubling operations also
      deposited their resultant slivers into canisters.

6)   Roving. A rove is a strand of fiber which has a slight twist in it. As one would expect, roving involves the creation of rove. The drawn and doubled flax fiber sliver was fed into a roving frame. On this frame the sliver was given its final draw and slightly twisted into a thread-like rove.

Principles of Spinning

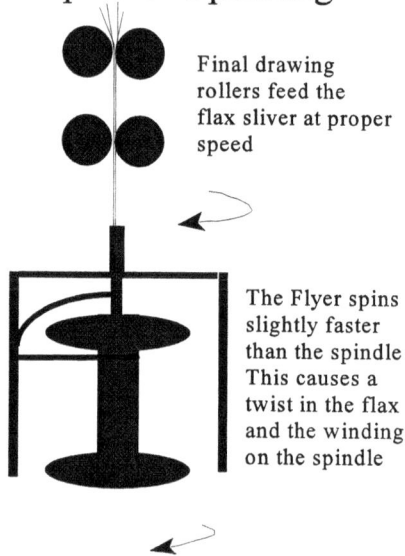

Final drawing rollers feed the flax sliver at proper speed

The Flyer spins slightly faster than the spindle This causes a twist in the flax and the winding on the spindle

This rove was then wound onto a roving bobbin. The roving bobbins of the double flange type were loaded in boxes when full for the next operation.

7)   Wet Spinning. In this process the rove was first passed through hot water at about 180 degrees F. This process loosens the gum that binds the flax fibers together. The rove was then passed through two pairs of drawing rollers and was fed to a flyer which accomplished both spinning and winding of the thread onto a spindle.

8)   Twisting. This process took several strands of the spun thread and twisted them together to form a plied thread. When done properly the fibers in the spun thread were made to line up in a formation which was parallel to the plied thread. This formation made the thread very strong and eliminated a tendency to unwind when under stress. In the case of shoe thread, five threads were twisted together to form a single thread.

9)   Reeling. The spun and twisted thread was wound onto wooden reels to a predetermined length. When thread is reeled to a predetermined length

(usually 3600 yards), it is called a hank. These hanks of thread could then be dried for immediate distribution or be bleached or be dyed.

10)   Bleaching and Dyeing. Flax in the unbleached state is brown in color. Most applications require that flax thread be first bleached. Often, as in broom twine, a color would be added to the fiber by dyeing the thread.

11)   Once dried the thread would then be rewound onto a spool for distribution.

What Was Made at the Dunbarton

The Dunbarton mill produced linen thread. Various grades and types of linen thread were produced based on the requirements of how the thread was to be used.

The finest thread was spun using a wet spinning process. This thread would be used to weave fine linen cloth. The Dunbarton did not manufacture cloth - only the thread which was sold for later weaving.

A dry spinning process produced a courser form of linen thread. This thread would be sold for the weaving of heavier fabrics such as linen towels.

Several strands of spun thread were often twisted into thick strong thread. This thread was used to sew shoes and other leather products. It was also used to bind the straw of brooms. Twisted thread was used to produce fishing nets (called gilling thread) as well as in the binding of books.

When the mill first opened and for its first 20 or so years, the Dunbarton produced many grades and varieties of linen thread. The types of threads included: thread for sewing machines and for woolen cloth, thread for leather goods and for shoe soles, waxed thread was used for shoe laces, sail twine, bale twine, yarn for linen fire hose, broom twine, fine colored thread, colored twine, yarn for fishing lines, gilling thread (thread for fish nets), book binding thread, carpet yarn, and carpet warp for further manufacturing. Finer thread could then be woven on a loom to produce linen cloth for towels, sheets, table cloth, or other fabrics to make garments. Around 1905 the Dunbarton was re-structured to put out the largest possible quantity of a few grades.

At the time the mill closed in 1952 only shoe thread and broom twine were produced at the Dunbarton.

Flax Dressers or Hacklers

At the time the Dunbarton began operation, scutched flax was the mill's primary raw material. This meant that the flax had first to be roughed and then to be hackled (dressed or combed) to remove the tow (broken fibers) and to separate the fibers. Roughing was done by machine and was performed by young men.

The hackling process was done by hand and required great skill. In Ireland hackling was considered a trade and required an apprenticeship of 7 years to become a hackler. Hackling was always done by men. Because of the skill involved, the hacklers were among the higher paid employees and were considered those with the highest status of a mill's manual labor. Hackling flax was very dusty work and hacklers were known to take strong tea or strong liquor at the end of a day's work to wash the dust away.

There was a custom in Ireland that was continued in the Dunbarton. Because the hackler's work was quiet, the men would designate one of their fellow workers as a reader. The reader would read the paper, or passages from the Bible while the other men worked extra hard to complete their own work and the work of the reader as well.

Back: George Ruddock, ?, ? William Reid
Front: ?, James Ryan, ? Thomas Wilson

The hacklers apparently amused themselves and others one January day in 1899 by holding a pigeon shoot at thirty-five yards. At some spot on VanNess Avenue William McCune, Thomas Wilson, Isaac Kinnen, George Ruddock, and John Giffin (all hacklers) released and shot at five birds. Only one bird was killed and that one by John Giffin. Two others were injured by unmentioned marksmen. In addition, they each took shots at a bull's eye at 100 yards. Isaac Kinnin hit the mark on two shots while the others shot completely into the air.

Like linen thread itself, hackling was protected by tariff. Undressed flax had an import tax which was ½ that of dressed or hackled flax. The following chart shows in various years the tariff and the amount of flax imported into the United States per year

Year	Tariff For Undressed Flax Per Ton	1000 Tons Of Undressed Flax Imported	Tariff For Dressed Flax Per Ton	1000 Tons Of Dressed Flax Imported	Ratio Of Dressed To Un-Dressed
1884	$20	2.37	$40	.96	2.47
1887	$20	4.65	$40	1.24	3.75
1891-1895 Ave.	$22.40	3.22	67.20	1.12	2.88
1895-1898 Ave.	$0.0	4.33	$33.60	1.67	2.59
1898-1914 Ave.	$22.40	5.51	$67.20	1.26	4.37
1914-1922 Ave.	$0.0	2.93	$0.0	2.10	1.40

As can be seen from the chart the ratio of un hackled flax imported exceeded dressed flax ranged from 2.59 to 1 to 4.37 to 1. In 1914 Woodrow Wilson made good on a campaign promise to establish more free trade and the tariff on hackled flax went to $0.0. On a national basis, this reduced the ratio of unhackled to dressed flax to 1.40 to 1. By the end of World War I, the Dunbarton abandoned the hackling of flax altogether. Flax was received by the mill from that date in dressed form.

By the end of World War I hand hackling was beginning to wane in other parts of the world as well because mechanical forms of hackling were developed.

The following were hacklers in the Dunbarton:

Edward W. Bennett	James Hume	James Quinn
Genie Bennett	Isaac Kinnen	Patrick Quinn, Jr.
George Brown	William McCune	William Reid
Bernard Collins	Samuel McDowell	George Ruddock
Robert Cordner	James McLean	James E. Ryan
Robert Couser	John McQuade	Andrew Sallans
William Davison	Bernie McReynolds	Patrick Smith
Robert Flemming	John McReynolds	John E. Walker
John Giffen	Wm J. McReynolds	Thomas Wilson
William Heran	John Nugent	

Preparing / Spreading

After roughing and hackling operations the first automated process in the Dunbarton was the process of preparing or spreading the flax. In the preparing room the flax fiber was thinned out, doubled and thinned out again to form a sliver of fiber ready for spinning. The following persons were involved in the preparing processes:

Isabella Curry	Susan McConnell	Celia Pagette
Elizabeth Clark	Katie Millett	John Quackenbush
Elizabeth Close	Mildred Booth	Mary Bolich
Sarah Corbet	Spider Hoffman	Helen Doole
Bella Giffin	Florence Kelly	Millie Welsh
Mary Giffin	John Kelly	
Sarah Hamel	Dorothy Kipp	Boss Preparing
Elizabeth Kopa	Frank Kopa	Sterling Berry
Rose Lowery	John Kopa	James Cooke
Ellen Lowery	Rachel Cooke	Harold Kipp
William McCune		

Spinners, Reelers, Rovers and Doffers

In the Dunbarton, as was the custom in Ireland, the spinning was done by women. This custom has its roots early in the history of the industry. In the 1700s linen thread was initially made in the home, the source of the flax was often home grown by the man of the house working in the field. It was then the women's responsibility with the help of the children to convert the flax fiber into thread on the wheel. The men took this spun thread and wove it into cloth.

When linen manufacturing on a grand scale began in Ireland, from about 1825 to

1850, it was natural to bring women into the mill to work the spinning frames. It was also natural to utilize the help of children in this process. They were good candidates for helping with taking the spools of thread off the frame. These were call doffers.

In a spinning department, each woman was assigned to tend to her assigned spinning frame(s). She had the job to assure that the thread was drawing properly through the frame and through the flyer to produce the spun thread.

There were two types of spinning. Dry spinning for courser grades of thread and twine and wet spinning for finer forms of flax thread. The wet spinning process required high humidity. It was the custom in Ireland for the women in a wet spinning room to work bare-footed because of all the water standing on the floor. It is not known if this custom continued in the Dunbarton. Overseeing the women was the spinning boss.

Other activities carried out in the spinning room include reeling. It was necessary after the flax was spun onto bobbins to then be reeled into hanks of a given length. It was the reeler's job to set up the bobbins on the reeling frame and run the frame the required number of rotations to create the hanks of thread. These hanks were then taken to the dye house or elsewhere for further processing.

After the doffers, the spinners were the lowest paid in the mill, the hacklers being the highest paid.

Betty Messenger's book <u>Picking Up the Linen Threads</u> is a superior work on what the life of a spinner was in Ireland.

The following persons worked in the spinning department:

Spinners	Charlotte Fletcher	Dorcas McReynolds
	Maggie Hall	Elizabeth Miller
Martha M. Bennett	Maggie Hazzard	Mary Moore
Enola Benway	Elizabeth Kelly	Martha Moore
Helen Blanchfield	Margaret Kimley	Margaret Mulligan
Jean Blanchfield	Marion Knapp	Lizzie S. Mulligan
Pearl Bowen	Vivian Lang	Rose N. Murphy
Henrietta Boyle	Mary J. Lyttle	Mary O'Hanlon
Margaret Bradley	Elizabeth Martin	Mary A. O'Hanlon
Catherine O. Burch	Mary J. McAllister	? Prentiss
Jane Chambers	Marg. McAllister	Sarah Redpath
Minnie B. Coffin	Mary McCann	Mary J. Redpath
Loretta Coumo	Sarah A.R. McCann	Mary J. Tomlinson
Maggie S. Dufrain	Maggie McHiggins	Dorothea Safford
Lizzie Flemming	Charlotte McLean	Lizzie Smith
Ellen Fletcher	Mary McNeil	Ellen Stargin

Elizabeth Threw	Susan Wolf	Jennie Giffin
Eva Woodrow	Anna Bennett	Lillian Brown
	Florence Burch	Sarah Richardson
	Clarence Ellsworth	Mary O'Connell
Boss Spinners	John Fletcher	Eliza A. O'Connell
	William J. Fletcher	Martha Emerson
Sterling Berry		Anna Brown
Patrick E. Fletcher	Reelers	Ellen Sallans
Allen Gravlin		Margaret Brown
Albert McQuade	Fred Babcock	Eliza Wilson
Patrick Murphy	Katherine Bennett	Katherine Wolf
George Ruddock	Sarah Birch	
	Pearl Bowen	Rovers
Doffers	Jennie Lyttle	
	Sarah Brown	Ellen Boyle
Julia A. Murphy	Jane Feenan	Mary Boyle
Evelyn E. Nolan	Dorcas Doole	Bella Giffin
Minnie Parker	Mildred Crowe	Mary McAllister
Helen Murray	Peg Derby	Marg. McReynolds
James E. Taylor	Tillie Doubleday	Susie Stover
Floyd Taylor	Dorothy Duket	

Twisting

To make thread for shoes and for gill nets and other applications which demand thick strong thread requires twisting of multiple strands together to form a single thread. The Dunbarton shoe thread was produced through the twisting of five strands of thread together. This operation was performed in the twisting department at the Dunbarton. The following people were involved in twisting operations at the Dunbarton:

Carolyn Bodenstaab	Diana Couser	Sarah McDonald
Pearl Bowen	Jennie Giffin	Sarah Meek
Anna Bowen	Lillian Brown	Ann Mullen
Celia Bungard	Sarah Lamphear	Jane McConnell
Jane Chambers	Fred Lewis	Frank Richardson
Hannah Chambers	Mary McCann	Annie Seeds
Ivy Cooke	Samuel McCune	

Winders

After various spinning, and dyeing operations it was necessary to wind the thread from one type of spool to another. Thus there were winding machines at various points in the process of producing linen thread. The following persons were involved in winding operations in the Dunbarton:

Martha Stewart	Isabella Hamel	Hugh Mulligan
Catherine Black	Ellen Pollock	Minnie McDowell
Vincent Carr	Emma Major	Lizzie Shilcock
Hannah Chambers	Mary McCann	Maggie Smith
Elizabeth Clark	Patrick McConnell	Mary Jane Stewart
C. Doubleday	Catharine Smith	Minnie Wilson
Lillian Brown	Sarah McDowell	Julia Wolf
Sarah Hamel	Lizzie Mitchell	

The Dye House Workers

The Dye House at the Dunbarton was actually a separate building attached by a hallway. The dye house was positioned so that the tail of the water wheel raceway ran under the building. This allowed easy access to fresh water from the river. Thread was dyed after it had been spun and reeled into a skein. This skein was then dyed in a large vat and once the desired color had been added or the desired bleaching had completed the skein would have been rinsed in clean water. The skein was then placed in a wizzer which spun dry the skein. These would then be taken to the drying loft on the third floor of the Dunbarton where they were dried. The following people were involved in dyeing operations at the Dunbarton:

Owen Murphy	James Cooke	Robt J. McAllister
James Shields	Samuel Crozier, Jr.	Arthur McCann
Robert C. Stewart	Samuel Irons	John McCann
Wm J. Tomlinson	Peter Lowell	Mike McCormick
George Black	James Majury	

Finishing Room

The final packaging and testing of the thread for shipment was done in the finishing room. The following people at the Dunbarton were involved in finishing operations:

George Brown	Tom Doubleday	Iva McMurray
Minnie Black	Vince Dufrain	Margaret Flynn
Ethel Conklan	Bridget Murphy	Thomas Quinn
Mary Conley	Mary Irons	Isaac Richardson
Edward Crossen	Frank McConnell	Lena Wade
Peg DeGregory	Patrick McCann	James Wilson

The Boiler House

The Dunbarton had two sources of power. The first was the Batten Kill itself. The river provided power through two water wheels. In addition, the mill supported a boiler room where a steam turbine was used to turn a main shaft. The firemen of the mill had the responsibility to tend the fire of the steam boiler. The following were involved in boiler room operations:

John Nolan	Joseph Brown	Samuel McCune
Benjamin Shaw	Samuel Crozier	Owen Murphy, Sr.
John Bailie	William Davidson	Owen Murphy, Jr.

The Two Master Mechanics and The Mechanics and Wood Turners

Despite the mill's long 72 year history the mill had only two master mechanics. The first master mechanic was Joseph Henderson. The second was George Jackson.

Joseph Henderson

Joseph Henderson was born 20 Jun 1852 in Bessbrook, County Armagh, Ireland. As a young man he was an apprentice in the machinist trade. Sometime about 1872 he started working for Dunbar, McMaster & Co. in Gilford. He soon became one of their most skilled mechanics and when Hugh Dunbar McMaster purchased the Greenwich mill Joseph was the first to arrive in Greenwich. He came in the fall of 1879. His job was to help set up the mill with equipment that was shipped almost exclusively from Ireland. Joseph was in charge of virtually every aspect of how the equipment would be installed, where the equipment would be placed, how it would derive its power, how it would be operated, and how it would be maintained.

Joseph was a man who liked to start things. In the spring of 1880 he helped organize and establish the United Presbyterian Church of Greenwich. At that time, many of Joseph's countrymen were arriving in Greenwich to work in the mill. Many of these people had been staunch Presbyterians in Ireland and wanted a Presbyterian church here. So by uniting with many similarly minded Greenwich residents, the United Presbyterian Church of Greenwich was established as a mission church of the Argyle Presbytery. Joseph would later become an elder of the congregation - a position he would hold for more than forty years.

Soon after his arrival, Joseph met American born Roanna Higgins, the daughter of Samuel and Eliza (Foster) Huggins. Samuel Huggins was also instrumental in the establishment of the church so it is easy to see how Joseph and Roanna might meet.

They were married in 1882, this being the first marriage between one of the Irish and one of the "natives" of Greenwich.

He was one of the first Irish to purchase a piece of property and build his own house. He built his home on Hill street across from the Catholic Church. As soon as it was possible to obtain citizenship Joseph Henderson made the trip to Salem with sixteen of his fellow countrymen and swore his oath to the Constitution of the United States in 1885.

He was a friend and counselor to his fellow Irish workers who regularly sought his advice. He always let his views be known. One Sunday, Rev. Paul Stewart was giving a "hell fire and brimstone" sermon. Joseph apparently stood up during the sermon and said something to the effect that Mr. Steward was out of place - and that sort of preaching didn't apply here! Joseph was also on the Greenwich Board of Education for eighteen years.

Joseph was no stranger to difficulty though. He lost his only son Phillip Henderson to the river on July 5, 1899 (see "Loss of a Little Child" on page 72). Joseph was right there when other mill workers pulled Phillip's body from the river. Joseph watched in agony while his co-workers tried unsuccessfully to revive Phillip. He never quite liked to see children around the mill after that. If one did happen by, he would greet him or her, take his pencil and give it to the child, and say "Away home with you now"!

About 1908 Joseph Henderson made a trip back to Ireland. While visiting his home town of Bessbrook he met a young man, who like himself, had apprenticed as a machinist. That young man was William George Jackson (called George). He told this George about opportunities in America, and specifically about Greenwich. In short, he convinced George to come to work in the Dunbarton.

Joseph remained with the Dunbarton until his 75th birthday, 20 June 1927, when he retired after 54 years of service. A year and a half later, he died on 6 December 1928 in his home. The community mourned his loss greatly.

William George Jackson

William George Jackson (called George) was born in 1884 in Bessbrook, County Armagh, Ireland the son of John and Sarah Jane (Walker) Jackson. In 1906 he married Sarah Swan Stewart in Bessbrook. In 1908 their first child William who would later be called "Stoney" was born. George too was trained as a young man as an apprentice machinist and he was recruited by Joseph Henderson to come to Greenwich to work in the Dunbarton mill.

With his wife pregnant, George decided that he should go first and Sarah would later join him. On June 26, 1909 George left from Londonderry, County Antrim,

---

Ireland for New York on the SS. Columbia of the Anchor Star Line. The ship arrived in New York on the 4th of July 1909, and he listed his mother, Sarah Jane Jackson of 2 College Sq., West Bessbrook as his closest relative. He also listed his destination as Greenwich to meet his friend Joseph Henderson. George then took the train to Greenwich from New York. It apparently had been a wet summer when he arrived. He related to his children that when he got off the train his feet sunk into the mud quite deep and he felt that he had gotten to the end of the world.

When George first came he boarded with his uncle, John Walker, on Bleeker Street. In a year or two his wife, Sarah joined him here. By this time she had two small children, William and Sarah. Apparently Sarah became quite seasick on the ship and the children were left to the care of others on the ship. Sarah was quite proud of the fact that she was able to sail in the cabin class and did not have to sale in steerage. Sarah and George rented a home from the mill on lower Corliss Ave right next to the mill. In fact, their home was owned by the mill and had been a farm house associated with the original mill property. Here they raised their children: William, Sarah, John, George, Dorothy, and Isaac.

George took his work in the mill very seriously. He was very dedicated and often worked during the down times to keep the mill equipment running at top speed. At the retirement of Joseph Henderson, George took over the position of master mechanic for the mill. George was very well liked in the mill. One of the machine operators related that while she was working he would always greet everyone in a warm way, and when she wasn't looking he would leave a dime for a cola on her seat. In his own quiet way he was able to make the mill a better place to work for all.

George loved to sing and was a regular member of the United Presbyterian Church Choir. He was also an Elder in this church and a member of the A. W. Morris Brotherhood of the church. At some point the family moved from the old farm house into the mill nursery (see "The Day Care Center" on page 126). When the mill closed George retired and at his retirement he was able to purchase his home from the Linen Thread Company.

George died in October of 1957 and his wife died in 1973. They are buried in the Greenwich Cemetery.

Mechanics and Wood Turners

Other mechanics who worked in the Dunbarton mill:

Fred Babcock	Harry Ferguson	James Mulligan, Jr.
James Doubleday	Ray Harrington	

In addition to requiring mechanics, the Dunbarton had a need for wood turners to

---

turn out wooden pulleys that needed replacement. Over the years the following were wood turners for the mill:

David Bailie	William Devine	William J. Hamel
John Gatherwood	James Doubleday	Robert Mahon

The Office Workers

The office of the Dunbarton mill was a busy place. It was here that the weekly payroll was calculated and distributed. In the early years of the mill, the payroll was done by cash. In later years employees received pay checks. The books of the mill were also maintained here. The mill's revenue and expense records were recorded and maintained in the office. All correspondence with the agents, customers, suppliers, the home office in Gilford, Ireland or Paterson, New Jersey, etc. would flow through the office.

The Office Workers: Standing: Cora M. Haverly, Mary I. Woodward, Shirley E. Garrett, Seated: Ida M. Flansburg, George Daisy, Violet L. Snell. Picture taken 4 Aug 1944. Picture in possession of Shirley (Garrett) Friday

The mill built a two-story building to house its offices in 1899. According to Shirley (Garrett) Friday, the payroll clerk sat just inside the office where he or she could deal directly with the mill's working population. The mill's manager was housed in this building, his office being a large room. The mill manager's secretary's desk was in the same room as the mill's manager.

Also according to Shirley, she was also responsible to test the thread. She would go over to the finishing department and put some thread onto a tester which would measure the strength of the thread.

The following worked in the mill's office:

James Bright	Cora M. Haverly	Violet Snell
Thomas Eddy	Allen H. Lewis	Charles VanKirk
Thomas Emerson	Guy McClarghty	Hugh Wallace
William Farris	Walter McCrum	James Wallace
Ida M. Flansburg	Robert McMaster	Arthur Wilcox
Robert H. Forsythe	Walter Shaw	Mary Woodward
Shirley Garrett		

The Management of the Mill

The Dunbarton was managed locally by a mill manager who oversaw all aspects of the mill and the office. In addition the mill manager was directly responsible to the board of directors of the corporation. When the Dunbarton became a part of the Linen Thread Company, the mill manager was directly responsible to the executives of the Linen Thread Company. The mill manager also had a mill superintendent

James Wallace

James Bright

whose job it was to see that the mill itself ran at full efficiency. Each of the departments, from the boiler room to the spinning room was supervised by a foreman.

The Dunbarton had the following managers, superintendents and foremen:

Title	Name	Years
Managing	Hugh Dunbar McMaster	Fall 1879 - May 1880
Director	John George McMaster*	May 1880 - Apr 1888
Mill Manager	James Wallace	Apr 1888 - Oct 1909
	James Bright	Oct 1909 - Aug 1915
	William Simms	Aug 1915 - abt 1916
	Arthur Wilcox	abt 1916 - Nov 1921
	Howard Anderson	Nov 1921 - May 1926
	George Daisy	Jun 1926 - Sept 1952

William Simms

Arthur Wilcox

* A. Acheson McMaster took temporary charge of the mill during the summer of 1883 when John G. McMaster and his wife spent about two months in Ireland.

Mill Super.	William Seaton	Jan 1880 - Jan 1885
	James Bright	Jan 1885 - Mar 1901
	Samuel Brown	Apr 1901 - Aug 1903
	James Bright	Aug 1903 - Sept 1909
	William Simms	Sept 1909 - Aug 1915
	Robert Heatherington	abt 1915 - Mar 1918
	Anthony P. Weatherup	Mar 1918 - Jul 1920
	George Daisy	Jul 1920 - May 1926
	Joseph Ritchie	May 1926 - 1952

Mill Foremen	Fred W. Babcock, John J. Black, James Bright, William Bright, George Brown, William Burns, James Cooke, Samuel Crozier, George Daisy, James Davison, Thomas Doubleday, Joseph Henderson, John W. Hogan; George Jackson, Arthur McCann, John McCann, P. J. McConnell, Robert Meek, James Millett, William Mulligan, Donald Perkins; George Ruddock, James E. Ryan, Andrew Sallans, Benjamin Shaw, William Simms, Samuel Stephenson, James G. Wilson, and William John Wilson

The Agents

As in any business, the life blood of its business is sales. If your product does not sell then you cannot remain in business. The sales approach for the Dunbarton under H. Dunbar McMaster was to sell its product through direct agents. Product from the mill was sent to warehouses and sold from there directly to customers.

Zell's United States Business Directory of 1881 has the following entry:

> Dunbar, McMaster & Co. Mfg of gilling thread, book binders thread, shoe thread, sewing thread etc. (John S. White, Sole agent) 106 Worth, Manufacturie, Gilford, Ireland and Greenwich, New York.

At the time the Dunbarton mill was incorporated in 1892 the following were agents of the mill:

New England District

> Warehouse and office, 25 High Street, Boston - Agent Zenas Sears
> Traveling Salesmen - Edward Loomas and Edwin I. Brown

New York District

> Warehouse and Office, 103 Franklin Street, New York - Agent Robert J. Wait
> Sub agent at 47 Chestnut street, Rochester - M. Adler
> Sub agent at 17 W. German street, Baltimore - A. L. Stewart

Western District

> Warehouse and office, 247 and 249 Monroe St., Chicago - Agent Robert Crothers

Pacific Coast District

Warehouse and office, 308 Market St., San Francisco - Agent T. W. Armstrong

Special Agencies

For Salmon Net Manufacturing - J. O. Hawthorn, Astoria, Oregon
For Glove Manufacturing - D. W. Anibal, 21 W. Fulton St., Gloversville, New York

In 1897 agents were listed in the Journal as:

Agents

Massachusetts
New York, 105 Franklin St. - R. J. Wait
Boston, 278 Devonshire St. - J. O. LaVake
Chicago, 167 and 169 Fifth Ave - Robert Crothers
San Francisco, 303 California St. - Eddington Debrick

Sub-agencies

Gloversville, New York
Rochester, New York
Portland, Oregon
Astoria, Oregon

The following quote from the Greenwich Journal of 15 September 1897 provides some insight into how the Dunbarton sold its goods:

"All orders from these houses [the agencies] are carefully filled and customers, no mater in what section of the United States they may reside can always rely on the ability and good judgement of the Dunbarton Flax Spinning Company to meet their wishes and demands in every particular. Mr. J. W. Wallace, vice president, treasurer and general manager gives his personal attention to all the details of the business."

John H. Wallace was mentioned in the Journal as the representative of the Dunbarton Flax Spinning Company at Lynn, Massachusetts. In December 1897.

In 1901, when the Dunbarton Flax Spinning company merged with the Linen Thread company, the Dunbarton relied on the agents of the Linen Thread to sell their product. The direct agents were no longer used.

Sources of Flax

Initially, it was hoped that the flax from Washington and Rensselaer Counties (see Flax and Washington and Rensselaer Counties on page 23) would provide the source of the raw material for the production of linen thread at the Dunbarton. The Dunbar, McMaster & Co. made many attempts to encourage local production of flax. Even before production began in 1880, Dunbar, McMaster & Co. advertised that they would import flax seed to support the culture of flax on nearby farms. They were willing to import Riga or Dutch flax seed. Riga was for light soil while Dutch was for heavier land. The cost per bushel was $3.50 delivered to the United States. In August 1880 the Journal reported that the flax crop in Greenwich was the largest in years. Also in August, Walden Eddy Co. advertised extensively for rotted flax - offering the highest cash price.

However, it was soon discovered that the best flax had to be imported. It turned out that the locally grown flax was of poor quality and was not suitable as a source for the Dunbarton products. The primary growing countries for flax were Russia, Belgium, Ireland, Finland and France.

During World War I the Greenwich Journal expressed concern about the Dunbarton's ability to meet orders because the war had made shipments nearly impossible:

> No flax is being shipped from Russia; Belgium and the flax-growing sections of France are laid waste by war; and the supply from Ireland is far short of demand.

During World War II the Journal once again wrote of the difficulty of the Dunbarton to meet the demands for linen thread because the sources in Europe were torn by war. In the fall of 1940 the supply was so undependable, the Dunbarton mill did some experimenting by preparing some soil for the culture of flax in the spring and summer of 1941. Apparently the use of a gasoline powered tiller was cause for quite a stir in town as no one had ever seen such a thing. The tiller aside, the Dunbarton hoped that a successful experiment would lead to a rebirth of flax culture throughout Washington County. Either the flax grown was not of good enough quality or the knowledge and technique of converting it from field to hackled form was poor, because it appears that the experiment was unsuccessful and the Dunbarton continued to be dependant on foreign flax.

Cotton vs Linen

As early as 1793, the invention of the cotton gin in by Eli Whitney marked a difficult future for linen. This invention greatly reduced the cost of producing cotton threads and fabrics relative to linen. It was primarily the low cost of labor which made the production of linen at all feasible throughout the 19th and early 20th century. The quantity of linen produced since that time has been on a steady decline.

Apart from the cost of manufacturing there are some significant differences between linen and cotton fabrics:

Linen	Cotton
Fiber has a natural luster	Fiber has a dull finish
Absorbs moisture very quickly	Is slow to absorb moisture
Does not soil easily	Soils more readily
Long natural fiber (3 to 36 in)	Short fiber (½ to 2 in)
Does not dye readily	Dyes readily
Has a natural stiffness	Has a natural softness
Relatively Expensive to produce	Relatively Inexpensive to produce

With the invention of the cotton gin, the American South converted much of its rice and indigo production to cotton. Much of the world's supply of cotton came from the South. The advent of the American Civil War caused a worldwide shortage of cotton. During this period the demand for linen soared as a result of this shortage. Those companies who were in the linen business became extremely profitable almost overnight. The establishment of linen mills in the United States shortly after the Civil War by the Barbours, Finlaysons and McMasters is a direct result of this prosperity.

Flax and Washington and Rensselaer Counties

Flax fiber production in the United States followed a steady decline until the American Civil War. During this war cotton production fell and the American North found itself in need of a substitute. Flax fiber production soared. A ledger book of Harvey P. Wilcox, who operated a flax mill near the Eddy Plow works in Greenwich, showed that an acre of flax sold for $22.50 per acre in 1863 and in 1865 the price was as high as $35.00 per acre. With this kind of a price increase it is not hard to see how farmers would quickly switch to this crop. This high level of production continued until about 1870 and then quickly dropped to below pre-war levels.

The following table from Census information is helpful:

US Flax Production	1850 US Census	1860 US Census	1870 US Census	1880 US Census
Pounds of Flax Fiber Produced	7.7 Million	4.7 Million	27 Million	1.6 Million

Long before the establishment of the Dunbarton mill, Washington and Rensselaer Counties were known as the seat of flax production in America. Greenwich, New York is located in southern Washington County and is located about ten miles north of Rensselaer County. These counties were renown for the growing of "North River" flax. North River flax was considered fine enough for use in the production of linen. At one time Washington County supported as many as thirty flax mills (scutching mills) and five oil mills for the production of linseed oil. It is said that nearly every small stream in Pittstown (in Rensselaer county) supported a flax mill. By 1880 New York State was one of the few states producing flax for fiber and New York accounted for more than half of the United States production. Also in 1880 Washington and Rensselaer Counties represented more than 40 per cent of the entire United States flax fiber production. The relative importance of Washington and Rensselaer Counties for flax fiber production can be seen in the following chart taken from United States Census returns:

Production Year	US Flax Fiber in Pounds	New York Flax Fiber in Pounds	Washington County Flax Fiber in Pounds	Rensselaer County Flax Fiber in Pounds
1870	27.1 Million	3.7 Million	1.3 Million	.8 Million
1880	1.6 Million	.8 Million	.3 Million	.3 Million

The original mill building, which was later to become the Dunbarton, was built in about 1869 by the Greenwich Linen Company. It was hoped that this mill would process the vast amount of flax fiber produced in the vicinity of Greenwich in Washington and Rensselaer Counties. This endeavor failed prior to anything ever being produced by the firm.

Interestingly, little of this locally grown flax was ever processed in the Dunbarton. It turns out that the qualities of local flax were inconsistent with the production of quality linen thread. By the late 1880s the production of flax in Washington and Rensselaer Counties completely ceased. The Dunbarton became wholly dependant on foreign supplies of flax. Almost all the flax used in the Dunbarton was to come from France, Belgium, Finland and Russia. This dependance did lead to shortages during both world wars.

The Flax and Hemp Growers and Spinners Association

Both Hugh Dunbar and John G. McMaster were active in the Flax and Hemp Growers and Spinners Association. This organization attempted to make improvements in the culture and processing of flax and hemp.

In July of 1882, John McMaster attended the Association's meeting in Saratoga, New York with Walden Eddy and Oscar Eddy. The Eddys' interest in the association came from the fact that they ran two flax scutching mills in Greenwich.

In February of 1883, John G. McMaster was elected as treasurer of the Flax and Hemp Spinners and Growers Association.

The organization was national in character and yet it held its annual meeting in Greenwich in 1887. At the 1887 meeting H. D. McMaster demonstrated a new fiber cleaning machine based on a French patent called the Cardon machine. This machine was more efficient than earlier scutching processes and created less waste. The Cardon machine could be attended by women and boys thus eliminating the need for skilled labor in the scutching process. The machine required 5 horse power which could easily be supplied by burning the straw produced from the scutching process. H. D. McMaster presented this in hopes that the production of flax fiber might be carried on in the United States. In 1887 there were 500,000 acres of flax grown in the western United States for seed production only. It was estimated that the fiber from this flax was worth $25,000,000 if only it could be processed efficiently. In his address, H. D. McMaster was attempting to eliminate the importation of flax from foreign sources and replace it with home grown flax.

McMaster had close dealings with the Barbours of Patterson, New Jersey as indicated by their collaborative work in this association. In this country, representatives of the Barbour Flax Spinning Company were active in the Flax and Hemp Growers and Spinners Association.

Chapter II - The history of the Dunbarton

General Time Line of Events

Date	Event
1768	John Barbour of Paisley, Scotland moved to Lisburn, Ireland
1784	John Barbour established a linen thread manufacturing concern. John had two sons John and William. William developed this concern into a large scale manufacturing business under the name of William Barbour & Sons, Ltd. William had five sons that he took into partnership including Robert Barbour and Thomas Barbour. Sons Robert and Thomas would later come to America and establish the American branch of the Barbour trade.
4 Feb 1836	Hugh Dunbar and W. A. Stewart formed a partnership and established a linen thread mill in Gilford, Ireland.
1837	W. A. Stewart died. Hugh Dunbar formed a partnership with Robert Thompson.
1839	Robert Thompson died. Hugh Dunbar formed a partnership with John Walsh McMaster and another with James Dickenson. Dunbar McMaster & Co was formed for the spinning of flax and linen thread while Dunbar Dickenson & Co produced brown linen. Hugh Dunbar was the sole owner of all the mills and mill property in Gilford.
1840	Thomas Barbour came to the United States
Nov 1841	The Flax Spinning mills of Dunbar McMaster & Co were completed in Gilford.
1847	Hugh Dunbar died. His estate eventually passed to his sisters misses Anne and Jane Dunbar.
9 Sept 1847	William Barbour was born the son of Thomas and Sarah Elizabeth (Warren) Barbour in New York City.
1852	Thomas Barbour began to import threads and twines to this country.
1855	The firm of Barbour Brothers was established when Thomas took

	on his brother Robert Barbour as a partner. The firm continued to import threads and twines from Ireland.
1858	John Walsh McMaster purchased Anne and Jane Dunbar interest in the firm of Dunbar McMaster & Co. including all property and mills.
1861-1865	A great linen boom occurred and the Barbours and McMaster families became quite wealthy.
1864	The Passiac Mill No 2 was purchased by the Barbour Brothers and using machinery imported from Ireland, production of linen thread was begun at Paterson, NJ.
15 Feb 1866	The Barbour Flax Spinning Company of Paterson, NJ is formed with Thomas Barbour as President.
1872	John Welsh McMaster died. Control of the Dunbar McMaster & Co. passed to his six sons. The eldest son, Hugh Dunbar McMaster, takes primary control of Dunbar McMaster & Co and title to all property and mills.
1875	Robert Barbour became president of the Barbour Flax Spinning Company.
Oct 1879	Hugh Dunbar McMaster came to Greenwich to purchase the mill which would become the Dunbarton mill.
Fall 1879	Joseph J. Henderson was the first person to come from Ireland to set up operations in the Greenwich mill. He had been send by the Dunbar McMaster & Co. of Gilford Ireland to install the machinery that was to be used in the plant.
15 Dec 1879	The mill in Greenwich was purchased by John S. White of 106 Worth St. in New York City. John S. White is Sole agent for the Dunbar McMaster & Co. Manufacturers.
1880	The mill in Greenwich was established. Workers from Ireland began to arrive in large numbers. Workers also came from the Paterson plant and a linen thread manufacturer located in Mechanicville, New York. John George McMaster came from Gilford to manage the mill. William Seaton was brought from Mechanicville to act as superintendent in the mill.
29 Sept 1881	Hugh Dunbar McMaster, John George McMaster, Percy Jocelyn McMaster of Gilford Ireland and then composing the firm of

	Dunbar McMaster & Company purchased the Greenwich mill Property from John S. White.
1882	Barbour Brothers of Paterson, NJ was incorporated with William Barbour, the son of Thomas Barbour as president.
Jan 1885	William Seaton left the Greenwich mill and James Bright became superintendent.
24 Oct 1885	The first Irish linen workers were admitted as US citizens at Salem, New York: Richard Kerr, Thomas Emerson, John Mulligan, William Mulligan, William Bright, John Ewart, James Mulligan, Robert Mulligan, Michael McDonald, William Herren, Thomas Couser, Robert Meek, William Devine, Joseph Brown, Joseph J. Henderson, Isaac Kinnen, Andrew Sallans.
1886	A limited liability company was registered under the name of Dunbar McMaster & Co., Ltd., of Gilford, Ireland. All property and mills of Hugh Dunbar McMaster were passed to the company under certain covenants.
1887	Katherine J. Seaton was the first daughter of an Irish mill employee to graduate from Union Free School
Apr 1888	John George McMaster returned to Ireland. Management of the Greenwich mill was given to James Wallace.
26 Oct 1888	The second large group of linen workers were admitted as citizens in Greenwich: John McCune, Robert McLean, James Mulligan, Peter Lowell, William John Wilson, William Tomlinson, William Davison, Edward Crossen, Andrew Couser, James Bright, and John Devine.
26 Nov 1891	The Dunbarton Flax Spinning Company was incorporated under the laws of the State of New Jersey. This company held all right and title of the Greenwich Dunbarton mill.
24 Mar 1892	Robert Barbour, president of the Barbour Flax Spinning Company, died.
11 Jul 1892	Dunbarton mill workers Ellen Jane and Frances Emerson, Jane Lowery and her sister Mrs. Mary Pollock, and Richard Richardson went over the mill dam in a boat after work. Ellen Jane Emerson, Frances Emerson and Jane Lowery died.
1895	Samuel Brown was the first Irish mill worker to complete high

school in Union Free School. He would later become a presbyterian pastor.

1897   William J. Wilson became the first Dunbarton mill worker to become a Trustee of the village of Greenwich.

1897   The Linen Thread Company, Ltd. was organized in Great Britain and The Linen Thread Company, Inc. was organized in the United States. This great combine established control of many Linen Thread companies on both sides of the Atlantic. The various Barbour companies were joined to this combine.

1898   John J. McCann was the first son of an Irish Dunbarton mill worker to graduate from Union Free School. He would become an ordained Catholic priest.

3 Jul 1899   Phillip Henderson, son of Joseph J. Henderson died after falling down the Dunbarton mill dam.

1901   The Dunbar McMaster & Co., Ltd and the Dunbarton Flax Spinning Company joined the Linen Thread Company.

25 Mar 1902   Thomas Barbour, the founder of Barbour Brothers died.

July 1909   W. George Jackson arrived in Greenwich having been recruited by Joseph J. Henderson as a mechanic. George would later become master mechanic.

6 Oct 1909   James Wallace died. He was succeeded as general manager by James Bright. William Simms became the mill superintendent.

by 1910   William Barbour (son of Thomas Barbour) was president of Barbour Brothers Co., The Linen Thread Co., Algonquin Co., American Net and Twine Co., Dunbarton Flax Spinning Co., Dundee Water Power & Land Co., Finlayson Flax Spinning Co., Hamilton Trust Co., NY and NJ Rapid Transit Co., Passaic Water Co., U. S. Twine and Net Co., W. & J. Knox Net & Twine Co.; and Vice President of the Barbour Flax Spinning Co.; In addition he was president of the American Protective Tariff League.

1914   Thomas Wilson was the second Irish Dunbarton mill worker who was to be a village trustee.

14 May 1914   The Barbour Flax Spinning Company paid $100,000 for the Dunbarton property, and business assets and liabilities.

| 15 May 1914 | The Dunbarton Flax Spinning Company was dissolved. The Barbour Flax Spinning Company was then taking full control. |

| 24 Jul 1915 | James Bright died. He was succeeded for a short period by William Simms as general manager of the mill. |

| 1916 | William Simms became ill with consumption and the mill was managed by Arthur Wilcox. |

| 1 Mar 1917 | William Barbour, the founder of the Linen Thread Company died. He was succeeded by his sons: William Warren as president, Frederick K. as assistant treasurer, Robert in charge of manufacturing in Paterson. William's fourth son Thomas Barbour, was a professor at Harvard. |

| Mar 1918 | Anthony P. Weatherup was the superintendent of the mill. |

| Nov 1921 | Arthur Wilcox retired and Howard Anderson became general manager of the Dunbarton mill. |

| May 1926 | Howard Anderson left his position at the Dunbarton to accept a management position with the Linen Thread Company in Paterson, New Jersey. George Daisy became mill manger. Joseph Ritchie was mill superintendent. |

| 20 Jun 1927 | Joseph J. Henderson retired as master mechanic at the Dunbarton mill. W. George Jackson took his place as master mechanic. |

| 6 Dec 1928 | Joseph J. Henderson died. |

| Jul 1931 | A branch of the Linen Thread Company in North Grafton, Massachusetts closed. The work was transferred to the Dunbarton and the Dunbarton mill went on two shifts. |

| 20 Sept 1933 | The Barbour Flax Spinning Company was dissolved. |

| 15 Dec 1933 | The Linen Thread Company paid $1 for the Dunbarton property to the dissolved Barbour Flax Spinning Company. |

| Fall 1937 | The employees of the Dunbarton organized under the CIO. |

| 1938 | Five O'CLOCK Whistle by Ramona Herdman was published. |

| 6 Feb 1939 | The linen thread mills at Paterson, and Kearny, New Jersey were closed by a general strike. |

13 Feb 1939	A strike was begun but only about ten of the Dunbarton Employees went out - not enough to close down the mill.
25 Feb 1939	Dunbarton Employees severed their connection with CIO and establish an independent Union with James Ryan as president.
19 Apr 1939	Strike was settled in both Paterson and Greenwich.
30 Apr 1952	Dunbarton mill was closed by the Linen Thread Company.
26 Sept 1952	The Dunbarton mill property was sold by the Linen Thread Company to Sherman Wiesen, Inc. Sherman Wiesen converted the mill to the production of tissue paper.

History of the Dunbarton Mill in Brief

The Dunbarton mill of Greenwich, New York was established by Hugh Dunbar McMaster as an extension of the Dunbar, McMaster & Co. of Gilford in what is now Northern Ireland.

In the fall of 1879, Mr. McMaster came to the United States to seek a possible site for a linen mill. The Barbour family of Hilden, Ireland had been very successful in setting up mills in the United States having established mills at Paterson, New Jersey in 1865. A high import tax on linen thread had made the establishment of mills in the States very lucrative. Mr. McMaster came upon a mill building in Greenwich which had been built in 1870 but the firm that built the mill had gone bankrupt before anything was ever produced. Due to lengthy court battles over who retained ownership of the mill and the lack of a good buyer, the mill remained idle for nearly ten years. Just two days before McMaster discovered the mill, Mr. Sprague from Boston had purchased the mill to produce leather board. McMaster, liking the mill and the village of Greenwich, offered a premium of $2,500 to Mr. Sprague. The offer was flatly refused and a premium of $5000 was countered by Mr. Sprague. Neither side would budge on the matter and Hugh Dunbar took leave for New York City with instructions to telegraph him if some arrangement could be made. Seeing that a linen mill, backed by the Dunbar, McMaster & Co., would be of great benefit, a paper was passed around the village and voluntary subscriptions were received from the citizens of Greenwich totaling $2,500. Mr. McMaster was wired on Saturday, September 27 and he returned to Greenwich on the Monday the 29th of September to close the deal.

Work was begun immediately on the canal and building. Bids were released to have an additional structure built to house flax. Mr. McMaster sent to Ireland for others to come help set up operations. One of the first to arrive was Joseph Henderson who was born in Bessbrook, County Armagh, Ireland. Equipment was shipped from Ireland and by June of 1880 there were 32 Irish families and 51 Irish employees working in the mill.

Hugh Dunbar McMaster's brother John was the mill's managing director until 1888 when he returned to Ireland. He was replaced by James Wallace who was born in Lowbrickland, Ireland. Mr. William Seaton was the mill superintendent for several years and was replaced by James Bright who was a native of Gilford. With the exception of a couple of years that Mr. Bright spent in Ireland, the management of the mill remained in the hands Wallace and Bright for over 20 years.

The village of Greenwich was transformed from having a few Irish families to having more than half Irish within a few years. Some of the Irish workers were to become influential business people in Greenwich (Joseph Lyttle, William John Wilson, Hugh Wallace). The Irish became active in local government by serving as village trustees (William John Wilson, Thomas Wilson, James E. Ryan, and George Ruddock). Two children of Irish immigrants became mayors of the village (Joseph Lyttle, Jr., and Jack Crozier).

During the Dunbarton's first thirty-five years of operation the mill was operated almost exclusively by Irish immigrants and their offspring (See the Chart "Linen Thread Workers"). Between the years of 1915-1920 there was a dramatic shift in the Dunbarton's workforce. All of the Irish families in Greenwich in 1920 immigrated prior to 1915. There are two possible reasons for this. First, World War I probably made immigration difficult. Second, James Wallace had died in 1909 and James Bright died in 1915. The mill's top manager became American born Arthur Wilcox. Arthur would not have had the same connections to Ireland that his predecessors had. During World War I the Dunbarton had difficulty attracting enough labor, so they built a two story nursery and offered day care to attract women workers.

Linen Thread Workers

Worker\Census Year	1880	1900	1910	1915	1920	1925
Irish Born	51	94	76	83	48	44
Irish Parents	1	10	18	13	20	6
USA Born	2	6	9	13	38	22
Other	0	1	0	1	2	1
Total	54	111	106	110	108	73
% Irish	98%	94%	88%	87%	62%	68%

The Dunbarton as depicted circa 1889 by Beck & Pauli

To maintain the large percentage of Irish workers required a steady stream of immigrants. The Irish workers and their families were known as Belfasters even though for the most part the Irish who came were from Gilford and its surrounding area, Bessbrook, and Belfast. Some of the families who came from the Gilford area include:

> Adamson, Bright, Brown, Carr, Chambers, Clark, Couser, Crossen, Davison, Devine, Duffy, Emerson, Ewart, Flemming, Fullerton, Giffen, Gilday, Getwood, Hamel, Heran, Kinnen, Lowery, Lowell, Lyttle, McCann, McConnell, McCune, McDonald, McDowell, McLean, McQuade, Meek, Mullen, Mulligan, Murphy, O'Hanlon, Redpath, Reid, Rocks, Ruddock, Ryan, Sallans, Sheeky, Shillcock, Steenson, Sturgeon, Tomlinson, Vaughn, Williamson, Wilkenson, and Wilson.

The Irish brought their work ethic, their way of life and their religion. The Catholic and Episcopal churches prospered on the arrival of the Irish. The Presbyterian church was established in the Spring of 1880 and two thirds of the charter members were Irish mill workers.

The hope to own a little land was one of the calling cards for those who came. Most families did end up owning their own home in Greenwich. The mill also built some housing for its workers. The design of these "row" houses was borrowed from the designs of workers' homes in Gilford with two rooms up and two rooms down. Many of the workers came and worked only a couple of years in the mill and then moved on to other jobs in Greenwich or even moved to other places. Still other Dunbarton workers worked for more than 50 years in the mill.

Mr. McMaster maintained direct control and ownership of the mill until about 1901 when he joined forces with the Barbours to form the Linen Thread Company. By 1909 William Barbour of Paterson, New Jersey was president of the Dunbarton Flax Spinning Company which controlled the Dunbarton mill. The Dunbarton continued to produce linen thread until 1952 when the reduced demand for linen thread caused the shut down of the mill. The mill buildings were converted to paper production.

1879 - 1880 The First Year

Date	Event
4 Sept 1879	The <u>Journal</u> announced that W. N. Sprague of Boston, Massachusetts purchased the Greenwich Linen mill property. This purchase included property on both sides of the Batten Kill, the mill, and water rights. He intended to move his machinery from

Bennington, Vermont to begin the manufacture of "leather board". He would employ from 20 to 25 people.

Oct 1879   H. Dunbar McMaster decided that he would like to purchase the mill. Sprague asked for an extra $5,000. McMaster agreed to give an additional $2,500 but would not budge another inch. Dr. Gray, a former Captain and Major in the 123rd Regt. volunteers, Mr. E. H. Gibson, Esq., an attorney in Greenwich, and Mr. J. L. Thompson, superintendent of the Greenwich and Johnsonville Railroad, started a subscription paper, each person pledging $100. In the space of a single afternoon $2,500 was raised in Greenwich to make up the difference between the parties. H. Dunbar purchased the property immediately. As an aside, Walter N. Sprague purchased mill property at Middle Falls, New York where he began producing "leather board" on 1 Jan 1880 (Middle Falls is a hamlet in the town of Greenwich). This man-made leather made from wood, flax and leather scraps was produced at Middle Falls for many years.

Nov 1879   Joseph Henderson, a mechanic who worked for the Dunbar, McMaster & Co. in Ireland was sent with much of the mill's machinery to begin setting up operations in the Dunbarton.

1 Jan 1880   William Seaton severed his connection with the American Linen Thread company of Mechanicville, New York to come to Greenwich to act as the Dunbarton's first superintendent. He reportedly was with the American Linen Thread (the American Linen Thread is not to be confused with the Linen Thread Company, Inc. in America) for nine years. He was given a gold headed cane by his previous employees. William was born in Ireland and had much experience in the manufacturing of linen thread.

Jan 1880   The first Atlantic cable message in Greenwich was received by Mr. Frazier of the Dunbar, McMaster & Co. The message arrived some time the week before 15 Jan 1880.

11 Feb 1880   Michael Dooley, night watchman of the Dunbar, McMaster & Co. mill, was apparently killed by a train.

5 Mar 1880   H. Dunbar McMaster arrived in Greenwich to directly oversee the setting up of the Dunbarton. He brought with him a number of hands from Ireland.

16 Mar 1880   Ten employees arrived: five men and five women. They were supervised by James Bright who had married just three weeks

previous. This totaled forty-two who had come. The following quote from the Journal is instructive:

> "If those who are to come are as intelligent and smart looking as those who have already come to Greenwich, we shall be glad to welcome them."

Apr 1880	High water in the Batten Kill was causing difficulty installing the flume and bulkhead.
1 Apr 1880	The Dunbar, McMaster & Co. advertised that they would import Dutch or Riga flax seed to support local production of flax.
13 Apr 1880	Six additional hands arrived from Gilford to work in the Dunbarton.
26 Apr 1880	Water was released down the flume of the Dunbarton and for the first time the mill was in operation. Fourteen more employees arrived from Ireland to work in the Dunbarton.
17 May 1880	H. Dunbar McMaster returned to Ireland. He left a very good impression on the people of Greenwich who wished that he would remain here.
24 May 1880	Fifteen more people arrived from Gilford to work in the Dunbarton.
2 Jun 1880	The Dunbarton Linen Mills [Fire] Company was formed with about forty workers as members of the company. See chapter "Dunbarton Fire Department" on page 39.
21 Jun 1880	John G. McMaster and his wife arrived in Greenwich. They took possession of their home on Academy street. Apparently the home had been made ready on their behalf.
Late Jun 1880	The first shipment from the Dunbarton was made. 600 lbs of carpet warp were sent to New York city.
1 Jul 1880	The Journal reported that the Dunbarton Linen Mill Co. were about to erect a large brick machine shop on their grounds.
5 Aug 1880	Mr. John G. McMaster offered a liberal reward for the return of his lost fox terrier.
12 Aug 1880	The Journal reported that the flax crop in Greenwich was the best in years.

11 Sept 1880   Mr. John G. McMaster and Mr. Robert Meek and others from the
                mill united with other men in Greenwich to hold a cricket match.

The First Batch of Workers

During the first year of operations, the greatest number of immigrants from Ireland
arrived. The following is a list of most of those who came in the first year:

James Bright	Margaret Kendall	James Mulligan, Jr.
Anna McDonald	David Kinnen	Jane Mulligan
Joseph Brown	Isaac Kinnen	John Mulligan
William Brown	Isabella Hamel	Robert Mulligan
Richard Carr	James Lyttle	Sarah Mulligan
William J. Carr	Samuel McAdams	William Mulligan
Lizza Devine	John McCann	Sarah Wilkenson
William J. Devine	Susan Hamel	James O'Hanlon
Maria Wilkenson	Michael McDonald	John Rafferty
John Ewart	H. D. McMaster	James Rafferty
Jane Fingerman	John G. McMaster	Owen Rafferty
Thomas Flynn	Catherine Gylday	Bernard Ryan
James Hamel	Robert Meek	Agnes Ryan
Robert Hamel	Sarah Meek	Thomas Ryan
Sarah Hamel	B. McReynolds	William Seaton
Joseph Henderson	Patrick Moles	Rosannah Sheeky
William Heran	Robert Moles	Thomas Sheeky
Thomas Hunter	Thompson Marrow	Mariah Thompson
Allen Kelly	Hugh Mulligan	Mary Ann Hamel
John Kelly	James Mulligan, Sr.	James Wallace
Mary Kelly		

Greenwich in 1879 - Just before the Mill was purchased

Greenwich, prior to the arrival of the Dunbar, McMaster & Co., could be described
as a typical eastern New York village. Its population was primarily composed of
people who were born in New York or one of the New England states. Most could
trace their ancestry to colonial times in America; there were a handful of Irish
immigrants, most of whom had come to work the lime quarries of the Lowbar
family in Bald Mountain, New York (Bald Mountain is a hamlet of the Town of
Greenwich).

In the spring of 1878 the bank located in Greenwich folded, causing great concern
and loss to the business community of Greenwich. It was amid this dark backdrop
that H. Dunbar McMaster arrived to put his bid in for the linen mill that would
become the Dunbarton mill.

The following is a summary of manufacturing establishments in the village of Greenwich in 1879:

1) There were four flax mills in the vicinity of Greenwich. These mills scutched annually 1250 tons of flax. Clearly it was hoped that this flax would be utilized by the Dunbarton mill.

2) Messrs. Palmer & Sons ran a knitting mill at the first dam in Greenwich. They were located on the Easton, New York side of the Batten Kill and produced sixty dozen ladies garments per day.

3) Messrs. Angel and Safford manufactured wall paper.

4) Messrs. Eddy, Reynolds, Langdon & Co. ran a foundry, specializing in the manufacture of farming implements. They were located at the second dam in Greenwich on the Easton side. They also ran two of the flax mills and scutched the flax from 500 acres of land per year.

5) Wm. Weaver's establishment produced Turkish towels and ladies cloaking. The Turkish towels were made by a machine of Mr. Weaver's invention.

In addition the following retail establishments existed in 1879:

1) Messrs. Ensign & Johnson were dealers in dry goods

2) Messrs. Gray & Brown were dealers in drugs and medicines. Dr. Gray was the Gray in the firm's name. He was a prominent physician and was partly responsible for starting the subscription that raised $2,500 to eliminate the gap between H. Dunbar McMaster's offer and W. N. Sprague's bottom line.

3) W. H. Hoyt, was a dealer in dry goods, clothing and groceries.

4) H. B. Tefft, was a druggist and a grocer

5) A. J. Bosworth was a dealer in groceries and crockery.

6) Leonard Cozzens was a dealer in large and model hardware, stove and tin ware.

7) A. J. Fenton & Brother, was a firm which began in 1837 as C. Fenton & Sons and dealt in furniture of all kinds. They also were the village's undertakers for twenty years.

8) Smith Brothers were dealers in dry goods, boots and shoes.

9) H. K. Cornell ran a livery stable which was established in 1845.

10) Corbin Dean kept four horses and a complement of vehicles.

11) C. H. Moore was a dealer in toys and fancy goods, established in 1839.

12) Alexander Arnold was the village photographer.

13) S. L Stillman was the village dentist.

14) C. P. Johnson, was a manufacturer of boots and shoes.

15) Stickles & Watson, was boss and jack of all trades.

16) D. W. Mandell was an insurance agent. He was also the police Justice for the village. He worked with H. K. Cornell, the lead of the police force.

Dunbarton Fire Department

In June of 1880, the Dunbarton sought to establish their own fire department in partnership with the village of Greenwich. On Wednesday June 2, 1880 an organizational meeting was held at 7:30 pm. The name was given as "The Dunbarton Linen Mills Company". The following were officers:

William Seaton	Captain
James W. Wallace	First Assistant Captain
Joseph J. Henderson	Second Assistant Captain
Thomas Ryan	Engineer
Robert Meek	Assistant Engineer
Robert Moles	Treasurer
James Bright	Financial Secretary
Henry Mandell	Recording Secretary
Samuel McAdams	Hose Foreman

The following committees were named:

Finance and Investigations Committee	Thomas Ryan, John McCann, Timothy Mahoney, Thomas I. Couser, John Hogan
House Committee	William Mulligan, Joseph Brown, John Rafferty
Uniform Committee	Joseph Henderson, Robert Meek

The following were members of the engine company:

James Rafferty
James Lyttle
Joseph Brown
John Kelly
Robert Mulligan
John Ewart
James Hamill
John Hogan

John McCann
William Mulligan
William Heran
John Rafferty
James O'Hanlon
B. McReynolds
Thomas Sheeky

David Wilson
Richard Kerr
Michael McDonald
Timothy Mahoney
Thomas I. Couser
William Brown
Robert Hamill

The following were members of the Hose Company:

John Mulligan   Owen Rafferty   William Devine
Thompson Morrow   Isaac Kinnen   Thomas Hunter

By 1885, it appears that John G. McMaster intended to get the support of Greenwich's three other fire departments because he presented each with a check for $10.00. He also indicated his intention to continue the practice of donating this sum to each company on an annual basis.

Floods

The Dunbarton's main mill was built in the flood plain of the Batten Kill. On a regular basis the mill was flooded, especially during spring thaws known as freshets. There were two issues to be dealt with during the spring: the first was high water itself; the second was the break up of the ice on the river. During some years the ice would break up in to large (9 cubic feet) chunks and come floating down the river. The chunks wreaked havoc on the dam and often would jam up and pile up at various points in the river. It was jamming down stream which caused the most issue for the Dunbarton.

Floods were a problem for the linen mill at Greenwich even before H. D. McMaster established his firm at Greenwich. Apparently the Greenwich Linen company, which concern built the original mill building, had a flood strike just as they were ready to begin production which caused many thousands of dollars in damage. According to S. J. Masters, who wrote an article in the Journal in May of 1880, this flood was in part responsible for the failure of the Greenwich Linen company.

H. Dunbar McMaster also got a taste of high water at the mill during his first year when in April 1880 the water was reported to be causing problems for those installing the flume and bulkhead at the linen mill.

One of the worst floods that the mill experienced was in the spring of 1902. In the fall of 1901 the Greenwich and Johnsonville railroad completed work on a bridge across the Batten Kill down stream from the Dunbarton near Middle Falls. The ice jammed up on the bridge piers and caused the water to backup to the mill property in Greenwich. There was so much ice jammed behind the piers that the bridge was toppled by the ice. The flooding that year moved the mill's hackle shop, a building 26 by 52 feet and two stories, including its heavy machinery, nine feet off its foundation and damage was assessed at $2,400. As a result of this flood the mill made structural changes to the banks of the Kill and the mill. In the summer of 1902, the Dunbarton had the rocks on the Easton side of the river blasted to widen the river on that side. Those same rocks that were blasted were then moved to the Greenwich side and a retaining wall was built parallel to the stream and downstream from the dam. The height of the wall varied from 12 - 14 feet and the stones were cemented together to form a watertight barrier to future high water conditions.

Other floods experienced by the Dunbarton include:

Date	Description of the events surrounding the flood
8 Apr 1880	The high water on the Batten Kill was causing problems for those installing the bulk head and flume at the mill.
11 Apr 1883	The Dunbarton mill closed because of high water.
12 Apr 1887	The river was higher than it had been in recent years. The mill was closed for a day or two on account of the high water.
27 Mar 1905	The spring freshet went through causing little damage to the Dunbarton. Part of the apron of the dam broke loose - total cost - about 50 to 100 dollars.
20 Feb 1909	The record freshet began on Saturday afternoon when the mill yard was flooded. Flood marks on the building placed the depth of the river at a full 15 feet above normal. About 170 feet of the mill's dam apron gave way to the stress of the high water. Two major sections of wooden and stone apron were found down stream from the mill. Advanced preparations assured that other damage to the property was not sustained.
15 Mar 1912	The river flowed through the mill yard for about ½ hour and the mill's basement was flooded. Preparation by the mill staff assured minimal damage was done. The receding water left large chunks of ice in the mill yard.
27 Mar 1913	A then record flood occurred without the ice jams below the mill. The mill was well prepared having moved all damageable equipment and supplies to a higher floor. The river rose above the retaining wall that was built a few years prior. The stream literally flowed through the Dunbarton mill yard. Little damage was done other than several wet basements.
4 Nov 1927	This flood, which was brought on solely by heavy rain and swollen streams from Vermont, was considered by the workers of the Dunbarton (many of whom had been there through its nearly 50 years) to be the worst in its history. During the night, the river rose at a rate of one inch every half hour. Several of the auxiliary buildings of the mill were damaged. About 300 tons of coal along with the back half of the shed which housed it were taken out by the stream. Although the flood occurred on Thursday and Friday, the Dunbarton was back in business in most departments on Monday morning.

Dec 30, 1948   In preparation for an on-coming flood, the Dye house was cleared on Thursday with work continuing through the night. The river crested during the weekend to 100 inches above normal, causing the basement of the main mill to flood. By Monday, the Dye house was back in operation and the main mill was working by Tuesday.

Law Suit

The 1902 flood was probably made worse by the erection of a bridge across the Batten Kill down steam from the mill. This bridge was built by the Greenwich and Johnsonville railroad amidst objections of the Dunbarton Flax Spinning Co. After the flood, the mill filed suit against the Greenwich and Johnsonville Railroad. The origins of this suit began in fall of 1901- before the flood. On 14 Oct 1901, the Dunbarton applied for a permanent injunction restraining the Greenwich and Johnsonville Railroad from building the bridge near Middle Falls. The reason for the application was the Dunbarton's concern that ice flows would jam at the piers of this bridge and the Dunbarton property would be at risk of severe flooding. A temporary injunction was issued against The Greenwich and Johnsonville Railroad on October 5, 1901. At court, an agreement was reached between the two parties when the Greenwich and Johnsonville Railroad agreed to put up a bond of $50,000 against future damage and on this condition the Dunbarton agreed to retract its petition.

After suffering the damage from the flood, the Dunbarton filed suit again and made its case before Judge Hand in court in early May 1902. The defense plead their case in the fall of 1902. The defense was that the Dunbarton Flax Spinning Company, a New Jersey or foreign corporation (by foreign it is meant a corporation which was incorporated in a State other than New York), had failed to pay its licence fee to the State of New York in a timely fashion. The defense argued that failure to pay this fee on time meant that the Dunbarton Flax Spinning Co. had no standing to sue in the State of New York. The deadline for paying the fee was 30 days after 1st of December 1901. The fee was paid and licence was issued on 16th of January 1902.

Judge Hand held in favor of the Greenwich and Johnsonville Railway on this defense. The Dunbarton appealed this decision and was successful in its appeal. The appellate court found that the late payment of fees was an issue between the State of New York and the Dunbarton Flax Spinning Company. The State of New York had issued a licence to the Dunbarton which gave them full right to file suit in New York State. The judgement was reversed and a new trial was ordered.

It is not known by the author what became of the case because no further record of the action was found in the Greenwich Journal. However it is likely that a settlement was reached out of court by the two parties.

Fire

Fire was something that was to be respected in the early days of the mill. Lighting for the mill was originally gas lanterns. The mill was powered by a steam engine which was powered by a coal boiler. Flax itself and flax tow or dust are very flammable indeed. The Dunbar, McMaster & Co. in Ireland had suffered a great fire in 1869 which caused £40,000 worth of damage. As a result, the company was committed to having a mill in Greenwich whose risk of fire could be minimized. Early drawings of the mill indicate the number of pails available for the dousing of flames. In addition, the mill formed a fire company early in its life see "Dunbarton Fire Department" on page 39.

Throughout its history as a linen mill, the Dunbarton experienced two fires. One of these occurred on 26 Oct 1898 when a small fire broke out in one of the rooms of the mill. It was quickly extinguished by employees of the mill. The fire was smothered with a fire extinguisher. Apparently the mill was very well equipped with these extinguishers. The second fire was also discovered in plenty of time to be put out by the employees of the mill.

One of the main reasons that the mill kept a night watchman was to assure that a fire did not break out and if it did to assure that it was brought under control quickly.

As an aside, the main mill building of the Dunbarton did see its destruction by fire. Operating as a paper mill under the name of Skybell, the mill was engulfed in flames on the night of 12 August 1976. Since this date the entire facility has been idle.

The Wind Storm of 1916

Sunday July 2nd 1916 brought some of the strongest winds ever experienced in Greenwich. The winds were so severe that it took more than 20 trees down on John Street alone.

At the Dunbarton, the flax store house had its roof removed and was almost demolished. Despite its brick and heavy lumber construction, the wind struck the building side, took off the roof and second floor; the whole building was taken out of plum. Slate from the flax store house flew and caused damage to other structures across the mill yard.

Upon hearing the news, employees of the Dunbarton quickly came and helped secure the flax in the store house. The water caused some damage to the fiber and a quantity was lost. The flax was quickly covered with canvas and on Monday it was moved to other buildings for safe keeping.

Apparently the mill had wind insurance to cover such a loss which was estimated at between four and five thousand dollars.

The Strike

There was but one strike by employees of the Dunbarton mill and even this strike was not well supported by most workers. All of the folks that I interviewed uniformly said that the Strike did more damage than good. In reality, the strike had a couple of outcomes:

1) The employees of the Dunbarton grew weary of outside unions and established their own union.
2) The employees received a 3% pay raise as a result of negotiations done as a result of the Paterson strike.

The following time line outlines the events of the strike:

Date	Event
October 6, 1937	The Journal reported enough signatures were recruited by the Textile Workers Organization of the CIO to establish a union at the Dunbarton mill. This same union had already organized the workers of the Paterson, New Jersey, Kearny, New Jersey and Anniston, Alabama mills of the Linen Thread Company.
October 20, 1937	A contract was signed between the newly recognized Textile Workers Organization of the CIO and the management of the Dunbarton. The contract called for a 10% pay increase. Representing the Union were Rose Murphy, Rachel Murphy, Julia Burns, Ina Chambers Theresa DeLongo and Raymond Quinn. George Daisy, Dunbarton mill manager, and Edward Last, personnel director, represented the mill.
May 25, 1938	Employees of the Dunbarton expressed concern in the Greenwich Journal that the impending reciprocal trade agreement between Great Britain and the United States might include linen thread and twine import tax reductions. Such a trade agreement would necessarily affect the marketability of their product and affect employment. This is because the labor rates were higher in this country verses those in effect in Ireland. The article recommended that the citizens of Greenwich should do any thing they can to oppose the reduction of tariffs on linen thread and twines.
Nov 17, 1938	The reciprocal trade agreement between Great Britain and

the United States was signed which reduced the import tax on flax thread and twine.

January 6, 1939   The Greenwich mill management notified union officials that the Dunbarton mill would no longer honor the contract and a wage cut of 10% would take effect on Feb 6, 1939. The wage cut was a direct result of the reciprocal trade agreement.

February 6, 1939   The wage cut took effect. The Paterson and Kearny mills of the Linen Thread Company went out on strike and shut these mills down.

February 8, 1939   Mr. and Mrs. Owen Murphy and Augustus Babcock went to Paterson to attend a Union meeting to determine what the New Jersey Union Employees were doing.

February 12, 1939   About 60 of the local Union employees met at the Odd Fellow's hall in Greenwich to discuss a strike. Some of the organizers of the Paterson walkout were also present at the meeting. It appears that most opposed a strike but there were a few who felt very strongly that there should be one. Apparently James Ryan moved for adjournment of the meeting but was unable to get a vote on this. At this point Ryan and three quarters of those present left the meeting. Those who remained distributed a warning to all mill employees that it would be best if they didn't go to work the next day (Monday). The mill management also distributed a notice that operations would continue uninterrupted as usual.

February 13, 1939   About 60 employees went to work as usual. There were picketers - about 20 of them - at the gates. These picketers included local strikers as well as supporters from Paterson and representatives from the CIO from Cohoes, New York. Apparently the actual number of strikers was only about 12 from the Dunbarton. To keep things orderly, Sheriff George A. Pierce and about five deputies (including James Ryan a foreman who worked in the Dunbarton) monitored the gates especially during shift start and end times. This event stirred great interest in the community. Apparently as many as 200 local people would go and watch the strikers at the gates. According to the Journal the sentiment of the community was clearly against the strikers. Since the local Union did not actually vote a strike, George Daisy, the mill manager, made it clear that he did not even consider the strike to be official.

February 14, 1939   A school bus was employed by the Dunbarton mill to transport those who wished to avoid the scene at the gates.

February 17, 1939   The out of town picketers left town.

February 20, 1939   James Ryan while monitoring the strike as a deputy sheriff was visiting the office of William J. Lyttle on Corliss Ave. He was showing off the tear gas equipment that he had when the canister accidentally went off. The Lyttle office was immediately evacuated.

February 22, 1939   All but 10 employees - mostly women - went back to work. Despite rumors that a large support contingent was coming from Paterson, none showed up.

February 25, 1939   50 employees of the Dunbarton met at the Odd Fellows Hall in Greenwich to: a) sever their ties to the CIO; and b) establish a local independent union. The meeting was chaired by Kenneth Kelly and Dorothea Safford was temporary secretary. Attorney John H. Dewell read a draft constitution for the union which was unanimously adapted. Initiation fees were set at $1 and weekly dues at 10 cents per week. The following officers were elected or appointed:

President:	James Ryan
Vice-president:	Fred Babcock
Secretary/Treasurer:	Dorothea Safford
Executive Committee:	Lillian Gravlin, Patrick Murphy, and Kenneth Kelly
Grievance Committee:	Kenneth Kelly, Samuel McMillan, and Viola Green Hoffman

March 6, 1939   "The committee of strikers" with Rose Murphy as president released the following statement:

To the citizens of the Village of Greenwich: We the strikers of the Dunbarton mill, are out on strike to offset an unjustified 10 per cent wage cut. The records of the company showed that the Dunbarton Linen Thread Company showed a fair profit for the year 1938 when other mills in the same industry showed a loss.

We feel that if this company can show a profit with the low wages that they pay us, we don't think this cut is fair.

The Dunbarton Linen Thread company in Kearny, New Jersey and the thread company in Paterson, New Jersey are out 100 per cent.

Not only eighty-three people but one thousand people. These people in New Jersey are striking to stop the unfair cut. And we the people in the Greenwich plant who are working for the same company are striking only to save that ten per cent.

Mr. David Malcolm, who is the vice president for the company, refuses to put this before an arbitration board because Mr. Malcolm is afraid to show the records or books of the company's profits which we, the union, already know.

Mr. Malcolm's attitude is that the trade agreement entered into with Great Britain does not affect competition or the unorganized shops are not competition.

Their statement is that the stockholders are not making enough profit on their stock.

We, the strikers of Greenwich, have the full support of the workers in the Kearny and Paterson plants and also the backing of the Textile Workers Committee of which we are a part. And any settlement that is reached in New Jersey will also be effective in the Greenwich plant.

March 8, 1939   The company's position was stated in the Journal. The fact that 70 of the mill's 80 people were working indicated general recognition of the fairness of the company's position. George Daisy was quoted:

Of course they don't like a ten per cent cut any

better than anybody else, but they understand the necessity for it. The company did not have a good year in 1938, but the balance sheet for the year does not show the whole picture. The reciprocal tariff agreement became effective January 1 of this year, and its effect was to reduce the price of our product.

George also indicated that average pay in the mill including foremen was about 50 to 51 cents per hour before the 10% cut.

March 9, 1939
Mrs. Ivy Brown one of the mill's non-strikers and Mrs. Alice Pettys a striker apparently became involved in a scrap outside the mill gates. Jimmy Ryan stepped in between the women to preserve the peace. Mrs. Alice Pettys filed third degree assault charges on both Ivy Brown and Jimmy Ryan.

March 10, 1939
An agreement was reached between CIO regional director Jack Walsh of Cohoes and mill manager George Daisy that the mill strikers might be able to return to work. Daisy agreed that the workers would be allowed to return and could be represented by the Textile Workers union of the CIO. Those employees who had voted a new local union were to be un-represented until the National Labor Relations Board (NRLB) takes action on the establishment of the new union.

March 13, 1939
The striking employees returned to work in the mill. The strike in Paterson and Kearny continued.

A jury trial was ordered on the assault charges against Mrs. Ivy Brown and Jimmy Ryan. The date for the trial was set for Monday March 20, 1939.

March 20, 1939
Judge Russell announced after jury roll call that Mrs. Alice Pettys had withdrawn charges against Mrs. Ivy Brown and James Ryan. The case was thus closed.

April 19, 1939
A settlement was reached in Paterson with the strike there. The settlement called for a 7% reduction instead of a 10% reduction. This same 7% reduction was offered to the Greenwich employees. Since the Greenwich employees had accepted the 10% reduction, the 7% reduction was also accepted although there was no one

union at that time to sign a contract with. The NRLB had yet to rule on who represents the Greenwich employees.

26 Jul 1939   Elections were held at the Dunbarton by the NRLB to determine who would represent the employees in collective bargaining. The CIO had initially resisted attempts by the Independent Union of the Linen Thread Workers of Greenwich, New York to be the bargaining unit. Despite initial claims of the CIO that the independent union was just a company controlled union, the NRLB held the election. The CIO seeing their case was lost withdrew from the running, thus the employees only got to vote yes or no on the independent union. All workers excepting office and supervisory employees were eligible to vote. When the vote was counted the 83 of the 93 voters present voted for the independent while 8 voted against and two placed blank ballots.

October 10, 1939   A formal contract was signed by the Independent Union of Linen Thread Workers of Greenwich and the Linen Thread company. The independent union had been recognized some weeks earlier by the NRLB. The contract established a 40 hour work week, one week's paid vacation, time and a half for work on Sundays and holidays, and guaranteed no reductions in pay scale for one year. The lowest paid employee made 37.5 cents per hour.

The independent union announced a celebration to be held at the White Swan Hotel on Saturday October 14, 1939 at 6:30 pm.

October 14, 1939   The independent union held its inaugural banquet at the White Hotel. Everyone had a great time including Sam McCune who was on duty keeping the boiler going at the mill. A meal was taken to him in the boiler room.

February 5, 1941   As an example of how well the independent union worked, the workers of the Paterson, New Jersey plant of the Linen Thread Company voted to oust the Textile Workers Organization of the CIO and establish an independent union on the same style of the Greenwich Union.

Cutting Back - The Demand Declines

In June of 1949 the Dunbarton was working a two shift operation, however its employees were asked to work only every other week.

On January 23, 1950, the Dunbarton mill went to a one-shift operation. It had run on two shifts since 1931. In making the move to one shift, the Dunbarton laid off 24 employees and had around 50 remaining. Those laid-off were those with the lowest amount of seniority at the Dunbarton. The lay offs allowed the mill to give full time work to those employees who were not laid off. Declining demand for the mill's product was the sole reason for the move to one shift.

In reality, the future of the Dunbarton was in serious question by 1950. With the end of World War II came a drastic decline in the demand for linen thread. This was caused by several factors. New threads had been invented including nylon. This fiber was inexpensive to produce. As the people of the United State became more affluent, the demand for shoe repairs dropped dramatically. Instead of getting one's shoes fixed, it was just as easy to get a new pair. After the war, the army changed the specification for its shoes to utilize linen thread only for the in-seam, other threads were to be made of cotton. It appears that almost all shoe thread was specified as cotton thread by the end of the war. Just twenty years earlier almost all shoes were made with linen threads exclusively.

The Linen Thread company did convert some of its production to the manufacture of nylon thread in its Paterson plant, however there was no attempt to bring this technology to Greenwich.

1952 - The Year the Mill Closed

1952 was a year that brought an end to an the Dunbarton as a linen thread mill. In that year the thread making equipment was removed and thread was produced no more. A few of the key events of the year include:

Date: Event

Feb 27, 1952   The Linen Thread Company announced its intention to close the Dunbarton mill effective April 30th. The news spread quickly as this announcement meant that the community would loose about 100 jobs with an average weekly income of $5,000. The Journal reported:

> ... the impending closing is distressing news from a financial standpoint, and also it is saddening because the Dunbarton has been closely allied with the growth of Greenwich

since 1879, when the mill was brought here from Guilford, Ireland, and when the immigration of Irish started, which continued over a long period.

The Dunbarton and the people who came here to work in that mill have unquestionably had the greatest single influence on the character and development of Greenwich in the past century.

It was announced that some of the employees may be offered jobs in Paterson, those with enough time will be offered a pension to retire and others will be given a separation allowance.

The mill's equipment was to be crated up and shipped to Paterson, New Jersey mostly to be stored in a warehouse. Local labor was to be used to dismantle the equipment, which was to be completed by the end of summer, 1952.

D. Leonard Malcolm, president of the Linen Thread Company wrote a letter explaining the company's difficult decision to shut the mill. The reason he gave was based on the fact that demand for linen thread was severely diminishing since the war.

March 6, 1952   The Industrial Committee of the Greenwich Chamber of Commerce, consisting of William J. Lyttle, Thomas A. Morrisey, William L. Sharp, and Kenneth Wood, met with George Daisy to arrange a meeting of representatives of the Linen Thread Company from Paterson, the New York State Department of Commerce and the railroad and power companies. The purpose of the meeting was to discuss the mill property and its possible use.

March 13, 1952   The Industrial Committee of the Greenwich Chamber of Commerce met with representatives of the Linen Thread company: J. W. Oliver, secretary and comptroller; D. L. Malcolm, Jr. vice president; and George D. Daisy, manager of the Dunbarton plant; and the State Department of Commerce; and the railroad and power companies. They discussed the future of the Dunbarton mill property.

August 6, 1952   The _Journal_ announced that operations would be ending within a few days. All raw material had been used up and the final work was being completed. At that point some of the machinery had been crated up and was shipped to Paterson, New Jersey.

August 13, 1952   The <u>Journal</u> announced that Sherman Weisen, Inc. would manufacture tissue paper in the mill. This was a great relief to the community that the mill would be refitted for a new use. Most importantly this new use meant employment for many of the village's working people. It was announced that the paper mill would employ about 125 workers. George Daisy remarked to the <u>Journal</u> that the Greenwich Chamber of Commerce was instrumental in finding this buyer for the plant.

The property was described as 65,000 square feet of floor space and five double dwelling units for employees. The linen thread manufacturing equipment was being removed from the mill. Sherman Weisen would take possession at the end of September.

Chapter III - Community Relationships

Attitude Toward the Irish in the Early Years

The population of Greenwich in 1879 consisted of only a small percentage of Irish born people. Most who lived in Greenwich could trace their roots to the New England colonies back many generations. Greenwich itself had been incorporated as Union Village in 1809, some 70 years before the Dunbarton began operations. To say that those who were here were an "established" people would be understating the situation. To assess attitudes towards the Irish who came is difficult because in many cases one must read between the lines.

Initially there was quite a bit of interest in the arrival of the Irish workforce. The Journal often reported on the arrival of new people. The reports only indicated the number of workers coming - not their names. The following example of this sort of news which was often reported:

> "We understand a number of operatives from Gilford, Ireland, are expected in town soon, and will be employed in the celebrated mills of Dunbar, McMaster & Co., of this village."

The following from the 18 Mar 1880 People's Journal clearly points out the general interest in those coming from Ireland:

> "This makes now about forty-two who have arrived to work in the mill, and there will probably be forty or fifty more who will arrive later. If those who are to come are as intelligent and smart looking as those who have already come to Greenwich, we shall be glad to welcome them."

Also in the 6 May 1880 People's Journal noted the outlay of money by the Dunbar, McMaster & Co. had spent bringing its people to operate the mill:

> " in the importation of a large number of trained and skillful workmen to attend to the mechanical department of their important undertaking."

However the Journal rarely mentions Dunbarton workers by name in the early years. The Dunbarton's "upper" class were exceptions to this general rule. Dunbarton owners (the McMaster brothers), managers (J. W. Wallace), and superintendents (W. C. Seaton and James Bright) were mentioned from time to time by name in the Journal. From 1880 to 1900 almost no obituaries were published for Irish workers. Sometimes, death notices were published, but rarely.

To read the personals section of the Journal in 1881 is not unlike reading it in 1878. The people mentioned and the events reported are more or less the same. This is in spite of the major shift in the population of Greenwich. It is almost as if the "established" population was just ignoring the new Irish population. The Irish workers were commonly referred to as "Belfasters" even though most came from the Gilford, Newry and Bessbrook areas of Ireland.

A few reports from the Journal indicate some negative attitudes to Irish people in general or to the Dunbarton's Irish in specific:

25 Jun 1883   -- Belfast On The Warpath - Lively Times at the Castle [the Castle was located on John Street and was an apartment building. It was recently occupied by Mr. and Mrs. George Jackson] - Edward Crosson was arrested Saturday night by officer Sanborn on a warrant issued by Justice Reynolds, on complaint of Mary A. Muldone for assault and battery. A few witnesses were sworn and the case was adjourned until Monday at 7 p.m. when the proceedings were resumed, and the evidence given fully warranted the Esquire in pronouncing the fine against Crosson for $15.95 and costs. The circumstances if we learn rightly, were that Miss Mary Ann who was boarding at Mr. Crosson's who resides at the Castle, notified Mr. C. That she intended leaving, and that she wished to get her clothing, etc., when Mr. C. Told her she could not have them until she had settled for her board, amounting to some $2 or $3. A war of words followed, during which Mr. C. caught Mary Ann by the dress about the neck, and shoved her about the room, whereupon Mary Ann, true womanlike, gave Mr. C. a blow over the head; Mr. C. in the meantime push[ed] and crowd[ed] and finally succeeded in ejecting Mary Ann from the room. A few of Mary Ann's friends came to the rescue and the matter of board money we understand was settled.

19 Mar 1885   -- The southern end of the village was the scene last Thursday evening of an encounter between two of the residents of Belfast, that throws the skating rink entertainments altogether in the shade. As we learn, two of the men employed in the mill, have been for sometime at variance,

and have not always manifested that Christian spirit due from one gentleman toward another. It appears that the parties on meeting hostilities were renewed; one gent calling the other a liar, coupled with expletives not found outside of Satan's dictionary; whereupon gent No. 1 administered a slight blow under gent No. 2's ear; gent No. 2 drew a large club, with which he was provided and gave No. 1 a fearful dig on the top of his cranium, inflicting a severe wound. Officer Fadden, being present, arrested the parties and took them before Esq. Mandell, and the case was adjourned until the next day at 7 p. m., when the matter was finally settled by one of the belligerents paying $3.00 and the other $2.50.

6 Aug 1885   --Belfast on the war-path again. A couple of Belfasters met in collision Saturday night, near Mrs. Liddell's millinery store. The disturbance was quelled before any serious results. The usual quantity of canal preaching was indulged in. Nice young men.

11 Mar 1886   -- An Irishman, being tried for assault and battery, in Virginia City, Nevada, was asked by Judge Knox if he had anything to say by way of defense, replied: ' Well, your honor, I saw but little of the fight, as I was underneath most of the time.'

The Greenwich Cricket Club

There is evidence of some cricket matches in Greenwich prior to the arrival of the Dunbarton and its workers. However, under the leadership of John G. McMaster and his brother Acheson A. McMaster, cricket was brought to Greenwich in a big way.

On 11 Sept 1880, a group of men from the Dunbarton along with many from Greenwich formed two teams of eleven players to play a friendly game of cricket. The Journal commented:

> We have among us one of the finest players in the United Kingdom, and we hope he may see sufficient interest among our players to be induced to take charge of a Greenwich "eleven," which shall eventually reflect credit upon our town.

The one among us was Mr. John G. McMaster who had the reputation of being the best bat in the north of Ireland.

In the summer of 1883, while John was in Ireland, Acheson A. McMaster organized a cricket club in Greenwich. Apparently Acheson had become a regular member of the Albany club and decided to form his own team based in Greenwich. Being a little on the bold side he then issued a challenge to the Albany team. The Greenwich club beat Albany two out of three matches in 1883! In early October 1883, the Greenwich Cricket Club was formally established with John G. McMaster as President and field captain, W. R. Hobbie as vice-president, Charles Griffin as treasurer, and J. W. Wallace as secretary.

The Greenwich Cricket Club continued holding matches for several years. They often held matches against Albany and New York City. In the fall of 1885, a cricket grounds of about three acres was graded, leveled and sanded on the Griffin lot behind J. G. McMaster's home on Academy St. This grounds was inaugurated in the spring of 1886 and was reported to be one of the best in the country. When John McMaster returned to Ireland in 1888, cricket died out as a sport in Greenwich, baseball having become more popular with the younger people.

Cricket Matches:

Date	Match
30 Aug 1883	Greenwich lost in double innings of play. The score was Albany 85, Greenwich 44. The game was held at Riverside park in Albany.
22 Sept 1883	Greenwich returned to Albany to play the Albany Cricket Club and was able to beat Albany in double innings of play. This was quite a success for the Greenwich team whose beginnings were just four weeks compared with Albany whose club was considered one of the best in the State. The score was Greenwich 63, Albany 41. This score is even more impressive because Greenwich was only able to field ten men instead of the usual eleven.
9 Oct 1883	Greenwich and Albany played yet another match. This time Greenwich won again by a margin of six wickets with a score of 65 to 71.
9 Jun 1884	The inaugural match between the Greenwich Cricket Club and the Albany Cricket Club resulted in a victory of Greenwich over Albany. Greenwich mounted 110 runs in first innings play while Albany could muster only 27. Albany made a gallant comeback in second innings play but could only come up with 39 runs.

4 Jul 1884	This was a big day for the Greenwich Cricket Club as it endeavored to take on the St. George team of New York City. Eleven of Greenwich's best went in hopes of taking on the big city team at their Hoboken, New Jersey field. In first innings play the St. George team soundly beat the Greenwich team 106 to 27. With the remaining time, Greenwich was able to acquire an additional 54 runs in second innings play at which point, time was called. Apparently the St. George club was one of the oldest in the United States and they played some professional players against Greenwich.
30 May 1886	The Greenwich Cricket Club married players defeated the single men 124 to 119 - a close match indeed.
8 Jul 1886	North Adams came and helped open the new cricket grounds which had recently been graded and seeded. The North Adams, Massachusetts team composed of Englishmen and Scotsmen fell to the Greenwich club 96 to 29.
23 Sept 1886	The Cricket Club went to North Adams Massachusetts and soundly won 110 to 59.
16 Oct 1886	The Greenwich Cricket Club held a match between its married and single members. Married won by a score of 70 to 68.

The following list of members of the Greenwich Cricket Club attests to the fact that Cricket was a sport which was enjoyed both by Dunbarton folks and by other members of the Greenwich community:

P. Bradley	Harry Gray	H. Seaton
James Bright	J. J. Henderson	W. Seaton
William Bright	W. R. Hobbie	T. Sleith
S. Brown	James Little	J. Spence
J. Campbell	Joseph Little	H. B. Tefft
W. Campbell	W. Mason	L. Thompson
A. Couser	M. McDonald	F. Van Kirk
Thomas Couser	A. A. McMaster	N VanVolkenburgh
E. O. Crandall	H. D. McMaster	R. J. Wait
Edward Crossen	J. G. McMaster	J. H. Wallace
A. J. Fenton	W. H. McNaughton	J. W. Wallace
G. Getgood	T. McShane	T. Weaver
J. Gill	Robert Meek	W. Weaver
N. Graham	H. Mulligan	A. Weir
C. Griffin	J. Mulligan	

Marches and Flute Bands

In September of 1888, Andrew Sallans and J. J. Henderson organized a party of about 40 from McMaster's mill, with torches, two banners and bagpipes for music. This party joined about 90 other young Republicans for a rally at the Opera House.

In October of 1888, the Dunbarton employees organized a flute band consisting of 16 flutes, bass drum and four snare drums. The instruments arrived October 30, 1888. Performances of the band were held:

Date	Engagement
24 Nov 1888	The Belfast Band made an excursion to Center Falls
18 Jan 1889	There was a major concert at the Opera House. William and Thomas Reid had been the instructors. Thomas Emerson read two selections of verse while Mr. Doubleday did some fine dancing.

Social Events Sponsored by the Mill in its First Ten Years

Nov 1881	Alexander Arnold executed a group photograph of 125 employees of the Dunbar, McMaster & Co. mill.
2 Aug 1881	More than 100 of the Dunbarton employees took a chartered train to see "Jumbo" in Troy, New York. The car was chartered by John G. McMaster for his employees.
24 Apr 1884	The Reverend I. N. Mulford delivered a lecture on sketches of scenery and social life in England and Ireland. The Reverend Mulford was brought to Greenwich at the request of the *Dunbarton Mills Literary Society*. His presentation was given at the United Presbyterian Church. This is the only event that I found sponsored by this literary society.
25 Dec 1887	The firm closed the mill for Christmas Day and provided a sleigh ride to Schuylerville, New York on Christmas day.

The Centennial of Greenwich

In 1909, Greenwich celebrated its first 100 years of incorporation. There were great festivities held for the occasion and most invited friends from other towns to participate in the fun.

Dunbarton flax Spinning Mills.

The Dunbarton mill from a 1909 picture directory of Greenwich, New York

The following were listed as visitors of Dunbarton mill workers in the 18 Aug 1909 Greenwich Journal:

Hosts   Guests

Hill Street

Mr. and Mrs. J. J. Henderson	Mr. and Mrs. Bullard and family of Schuylerville, and Mr. and Mrs. Robert Henderson of Valley Falls
Mr. and Mrs. Joseph Chambers	Mrs. Whiteside and Miss Blanche Whiteside of Amsterdam
Mr. and Mrs. Thomas Doubleday	Thomas Doubleday, Jr.
Mr. and Mrs. John Lyttle	Miss Nellie Lyttle and Miss Knack, Amsterdam; Mr. and Mrs. William Brophy and son Harold, Corinth; Mrs. Randall, Corinth
Mr. and Mrs. Tomlinson	Robert Tomlinson, Little Falls
Mr. and Mrs. William Mulligan	Mr. Hogan, Clark's Mills
Mr. and Mrs. George Brown	Mr. and Mrs. William Dittay and daughter and Mr. and Mrs. John Garvey and son, Paterson; Mr. and Mrs. David Boyent, Troy; Mr. and Mrs. Mosher, East Greenwich.
Mr. and Mrs. Thomas Corcans	Mary Henley and Richard Henley, Lansingburg
Mrs. Thomas Wilson	Mrs. Ellen Campbell and Mrs. H. F. Burns, Schenectady; Mrs. Elizabeth J. Douglass, Troy; Mr. and Mrs. John Campbell, West Hebron

Bleeker Street

Mrs. Marshal Stewart

Mr. and Mrs. George Ruddock

William Devine

Mr. and Mrs. Almy and daughter Mrs. Healey, Schuylerville; Samuel McDowell, Amsterdam.

Mr. and Mrs. Goodrich and daughter, Blanche, Stillwater

Mr. & Mrs. Rafferty & family, Paterson, NJ

Easton Side

Mr. and Mrs. Arthur Gravlin

Mr. and Mrs. Martin McNamara, New York; Mr. and Mrs. Frank Cathcart, Granville; George Loop, Troy.

Academy Street

Mrs. Margaret Brown

Mr. and Mrs. Lewis Lane

Mr. and Mrs. Robert Emerson

Mr. and Mrs. John Geer and daughter, Sandy Hill; Mr. and Mrs. Andrew McBride

Mrs. George Wright and Mrs. Schuyler Wright, Amsterdam

Mr. and Mrs. Robert Rogers, Valley Falls

Washington Street

Mrs. Sarah Herdman

Mr. and Mrs. John Mulligan

Mr. and Mrs. Hammill

Mr. and Mrs. James Bright

Mrs. Mary Millett

Mrs. Fred Babcock

Mrs. Davis and Mrs. Hughes, Troy.

Mr. and Mrs. J. A. Siclken, New York

William and Robert Hammil, Amsterdam

Mr. Pauley, Miss Pauley, and Henry Pauley, Brooklyn

Mrs. Shannon and son, Brewster, New York; Mr. and Mrs. Harry Millett, Mechanicville; Mrs. Burns, Hoosick Falls

Mrs. Robert Mulligan, Amsterdam; Mrs. Fred Jeffords, Thomas Jeffords, and wife, Schuylerville; Mary Jeffords, Saratoga; Thomas Mabee and family, Bacon Hill; Mrs. Gertrude Vandenburg, Gansevoort, Mr. and Mrs. John Crandall, Bemis Heights, John Jeffords, Gurn Springs; Mr. and Mrs. J. P. Gorham and family, Saratoga.

John Street

Mrs. McWilliams

Mrs. John Bailey

Mr. Brouflett, Miss Higginson, Cohoes

Mrs. David Williamson and family, Mr. and Mrs. Peter Williamson, Albany

| Mr. and Mrs. Peter Lesson | Richard Dornan, Mulberry, Massachusetts.; Frank Lesson, Schaghticoke; Mrs. James Hanley, Mechanicville |

VanNess Ave

| Mr. and Mrs. Archie Weir | Mr. and Mrs. James Lyttle and son Thomas; Mrs. Thomas Rogers, Mrs. John Lyttle, and Mrs. Robert Mulligan, Amsterdam. |

Elm Avenue

| Mr. and Mrs. Arch Daisy | Miss Ella Daisy, Glens Falls |

Corliss Ave

| John McCann | Rev. John McCann, Albany; William McCann, Schenectady. |
| James W. Wallace | John Wallace and family and Samuel Wallace and family, Gloversville. |

Cottage Street

| Mr. and Mrs. Ezra McClaughry | Miss Maria Rood, Eagle Bridge; Miss Grace Gilchrist, East Greenwich. |
| Mr. and Mrs. A. H. Wilcox | Mr. and Mrs. Edwin Wilcox and son, Newark, New Jersey |

The listing of visitors speaks greatly to the times. In 1909, the Journal kept track of the comings and goings of most folks. The fact that this kind of information would be printed for public use is in itself an amazing thing. Today, people value their privacy too much to want this sort of thing published.

It is also worth noting that by 1909, the linen mill workers were listed as hosts just like all the others. This is significant because it meant acceptance. From 1880 to 1900 the Dunbarton workers are rarely mentioned by name in the Journal. They were referred to as a class as "Belfasters". Obituaries for mill workers are almost non-existent in this time period of 1880 to 1900. From 1900 to 1909 the amount of material written in the Journal about individuals increased significantly and obituaries were regularly recorded for mill workers.

Italian and Irish Disagreements

In the 1910s several Italian families settled in Greenwich and many contributed workers to the Dunbarton work force. There were several incidences of violence between this new population and the "established" Irish population:

Date   Incident

20 Apr 1916   Tony Falco, apparently while waiting for the trolley overheard George Weir say that there was no room on the trolley anymore because of the "Dagos". Tony took exception to this and argued with George Weir. Eventually, Tony pulled a knife out and stabbed George Weir, just as the trolley pulled up. No-one thought too much of the incident as everyone but Weir and Falco boarded the trolley and went on their way. Falco fled and was never found. George went to doctor Rogers for treatment and apparently bled to death.

There were many prevailing attitudes against the Italian population. The following quote from the Journal at the time of the incident shows just how deep these general attitudes were:

There are no indications that Falco is likely to be brought to justice for the killing of Weir. So far as can be ascertained not a trace of him [Falco] has been reported since he ran from the scene of the stabbing, Thursday morning, April 20th. The authorities have never seemed very sanguine of the prospects of catching him, as they say Italian settlements are numerous and excellent hiding places for criminals of that nationality. Their fellow-countrymen keep their secrets well and means are readily found if necessary to take them quietly out of the country.

7 May 1916   Michael Denaro known as "Mike Black" was held in the Greenwich jail on charges of assault against James Weir. Apparently Denaro and another fellow were fighting when Weir and Patrick McCann came along and attempted to break up the fight. Denaro apparently struck Weir with a rock in the face.

Prosperity of the Mill and Greenwich

Although the Dunbarton did have its ups and downs in production throughout its 72 year history it always remained open. During poor economic times the mill would operate on part time verses shutting down. This resulted in fairly consistent income for a large population in Greenwich. The following are examples of prosperous times for the mill:

Date	Description of the time
May 1881	The Dunbarton was awarded a large contract to supply all threads and gilling twine to the United Stated Indian commission. This contract was won against significant competition in a difficult market.
27 Oct 1881	The <u>Journal</u> reported that the Dunbarton was three months behind in filling its orders. This backlog existed even though the order for the Indian commission had been fulfilled. In order to meet this three month backlog the mill had wired Gilford requesting additional machinery and additional workers.
Jan 1882	The Dunbarton was receiving orders for its threads and twines from as far away as San Francisco.
May 1882	The Dunbarton received large repeat orders. It was reported that the mill was producing a large order for the California market. The mill's superior quality production provided consistent employment while other mills in Greenwich were not running at capacity.
Jun 1884	The Interior Department of the United States government awarded to the Dunbarton, for the fourth year in a row, its contract to supply linen thread to American Indians. This the mill won in spite of the desire for several other competitors for the business.
Feb 1886	Dunbar, McMaster & Co. workers are compelled to work overtime in order to fulfill its commitments. The mill even had to decline some orders, and had been able to sell some of its product at advance prices.
Mar 1899	The Dunbarton expanded its operation by adding additional spinning capability due to increased demand for the product of the mill.

<u>The Greenwich Journal</u> often commented on how consistently prosperous the Dunbarton was. In April of 1908 the Journal reported:

"The Dunbarton company, which has for twenty years or more been the most constantly prosperous of all the local industries is also working to its fullest capacity, and probably never before in its history has the output been as large as it is now."

When World War I made access to imported flax uncertain the Journal reported:

"It is much hoped that the difficulty [in obtaining foreign flax] may be overcome, as the shutting down of this mill, if it should be necessary, could be a serious blow to the prosperity of the town."

In 1931, when the rest of the United States was deep in a recession, called the great depression, the Dunbarton went to two shifts and added workers to its payroll. This was indeed a blessing to Greenwich. With the addition of nearly 35 more jobs, about 25 were for women. To improve efficiency of its operations, the Linen Thread Company moved the work from its North Grafton, Massachusetts plant (Finlayson Flax Spinning Company) to Greenwich. Several families (most notably the Nolan and the Kopa families) moved to Greenwich from North Grafton to help fill the open positions.

While giving a brief history of the Dunbarton in May 1945, the Journal indicated that the Dunbarton had never been closed for more than a couple of days in its 65 year history.

In January 1950 the Dunbarton cut back to a one shift operation. At this time there were about 74 employees. In cutting back the Dunbarton reduced its staff from 74 to about 50. Since June of the prior year the Dunbarton had its employees working every other week.

There are a few instances where the mill did go on a reduced schedule due to slow demand:

Jul 1885   The mill shut down for 3 days.

1893   This year was one of depression for the linen business world wide.

6 Aug 1896 The mill was run on a 4 day week. This slowdown was short lived and in October the Journal reported the mill was back on full time.

1 Jun 1913 The Dunbarton went to a 40 hour week from its normal 54 hour schedule. It was a matter of concern both to the operatives and to the village because this mill rarely had cut back its production.

Alcohol

It may be safely said that anyone who has Irish blood has a special relationship to alcohol. Greenwich, because of the significant number of people of Irish ancestry, has a significant number of people whose lives have been affected by the use and abuse of alcohol. With almost no exception, those who I interviewed to write this history had an example of someone in their family who was alcoholic.

One often thinks that an alcoholic person does not work and just wastes away on the street corner. This is a totally inaccurate picture of most who were alcoholic in Greenwich. The average alcoholic who worked in the Dunbarton was one who:

      1) Never or rarely missed work because of drink,
      2) Was never in trouble with the law,
      3) Was a very respected person in the community, and
      4) Was very committed to their family.

When the Dunbarton first was established by the Dunbar, McMaster & Co., the temperance movement was in full swing. Public intoxication was punishable with fines as great as $4.25. This was a stiff fine in the days when a day's labor only brought $1 for a man. Still in 1880 there were many places in town where a drink could be legally obtained.

One of the mill's first employees, Michael Dooley, died while intoxicated, possibly by being hit by a train. Michael was night watchman at the mill in February 1880 - even before the mill began production. He was seen by several people to be drunk on the evening of 11 Feb 1880. He was found on the morning of 12 Feb 1880 lying dead across the tracks of the Greenwich and Johnsonville railroad bridge which connected the Greenwich and Easton sides of the village. He may have been hit by the evening train while using the bridge to return to his home on the Easton side.

James Lyttle, one of the first workers to come to Greenwich from Ireland, was arrested for assault and battery and for riot and disorderly conduct on Sunday afternoon, 26 Sept 1880. He was charged $5.00 and was forced to take the "blue ribbon pledge" and keep it for one year. The blue ribbon pledge was a vow sponsored by the Women's Christian Temperance Union or W.C.T.U. to encourage abstinence from drinking. The Journal noted concerning the incident:

> "It is time that this public desecration of the Sabbath on the public streets by drunken men and rowdies was checked, and we are pleased to note that the authorities are moving in the matter."

Throughout the Dunbarton's history, Greenwich went through periods of being "dry" which meant that no one could sell alcohol within the village limits. During the prohibition times, alcohol was illegal to be sold anywhere in the United States.

It is not known by this author the effect these periods of drought might have had on the Dunbarton's working population.

Drink habits of people who lived many generations ago are hard to ascertain but a few comments from people are quite instructive.

"Jim never used to drink in town. He would never want anyone to know that he drank. He used to go to Schuylerville and drink there."

"I used to have to retrieve my father from the Bar often."

"I used to hate holidays because that was when my father drank. He was the type who would get mean when he drank. He used to pull out the shot gun and threaten to kill a neighbor after he had too much to drink."

"We would call Dr. Skinner to come and give him a shot to put him to sleep so he could sleep off his drunkenness."

"Boy my father could put it away. All his friends did the same - but none of 'em was ever arrested for what they did."

"I remember running into George and Jim behind the barn. They were having quite a good time sipping from a bottle of booze."

"My uncle had quite a drinking problem. We used to try to keep him away from the bottle, but in the end he was always able to find some."

"The Catholics just went to confession so they could do the same [drink] all over again. It was the same with us protestants, we just skipped the confession and became high brow tea tottlers all week and drank all weekend."

Five O'Clock Whistle - Its Parallel

In 1938 Ramona Herdman published a book called Five O'Clock Whistle. This is a novel about a boy named David Lyttle. The story begins with David, a young boy, waking up to the stream of people who pass his house each day on their way to the mill. The mill produces linen thread. The workers were for the most part Irish. David's own parents worked for the Irish company and came to set up operations in the Dye house. His family came in hopes for a piece of land and a place to call home. This land they found, but with it came a mortgage. The story ends with the establishment of a union in the mill.

Although Five O'Clock Whistle is a novel, and as such it is fictional, much of the story parallels the story of the Dunbarton. Ramona Herdman, the author, is the daughter of Thomas and Sarah (Mulligan) Herdman. She was born in Greenwich and graduated from the high school in 1919. Her grandfather James Mulligan brought his family to Greenwich from Gilford in 1880. Ramona's mother, her aunt Mary, her uncles James, William, John, Robert, and Hugh all worked in the Dunbarton.

Some elements of Five O'Clock Whistle which I believe accurately represent the way of life that the Irish linen workers brought to Greenwich include:

1) A belief in the promised land. Ramona explores this idea in many ways. She defines the promised land as the land that was promised the workers by the owner of the mill as encouragement to come to work the mill. In this story the land was given free, but the workers had to go to the Bank for a mortgage to build a home on the land.

The promised land for Ramona is the hope that drove the Irish immigrants here, and the hope that lived on. For the characters in her story the promised land was both a blessing and a curse. The blessing was the purpose the land gave to life while the curse was the station in life that the promised land tied you to.

In Greenwich parts of Bleeker, John, Washington, VanNess, and Hill streets were considered by many to be the promised land. It is where most of the Irish did settle. In 1897 VanNess avenue was even referred to as "Promised Land" street in the Journal. When the mill first opened, these streets were mostly empty fields waiting for someone to build on them. It is not likely that the mill gave land away. In fact, any who were able to obtain property did so through their own purchases.

Others in Greenwich, perhaps with more of a bitter view, considered Gray Avenue to be the promised land which no one ever received for free and no mill worker ever could afford.

2) A belief that you can be as good as any of them, as good as the mill owner/manager himself. Much of Five O'Clock Whistle deals with the idea that through hard work, one could improve oneself. All one needs to do is let nothing interfere with one's determination to succeed. In the story there are clear lines between the workers who live and work according to one set of rules and the people of money who live and work according to a different set of rules. The book shows how difficult it was to cross these lines, but that the lines could be crossed. This belief is very strong in Greenwich.

According to the story, life was better here than it could have ever been in the old country. Though work was just as difficult here, there was a hope of doing better. The workers in the story saw their lives as much better off than the lives of their parents.

3)   There is in this story a strong element of sacrifice. As a way of living out the hope given through the promised land, the characters sacrifice their own life to the future of their children's lives. In the story, the first generation of immigrants had begun their work at ages as young as 9 or 10 because their family absolutely needed the additional money. At least here work did not begin until age 13 or 14. Each family was willing to sacrifice to see that one of its members go out and made something of him or herself.

In Greenwich, while many of the workers children went to work as soon as it was legal for them to do so, other families saw to it that their children got through school and on to trade school or even college. These things did not come without sacrifice on those who made it possible.

4)   Even though the mill defined why the people were here and it provided a way for them to live, it was the five o'clock whistle that set them free. The mill was both a steady rock on which to stand, something that always was there, and it was something to rise above, something to get away from for good. "You don't want to be working in a mill all your life" seems to be the moral of the story.

This feeling was also strong in Greenwich. While the workers at the Dunbarton did dedicate many years of their own lives to the mill, they often encouraged their own children to pursue other opportunities.

Some of the key characters in the story:

David Lyttle	It was from his perspective the story is told. His story begins at about age 9 and continues to about age 25. He was good at school and also becomes a good singer. It was the sacrifice of his parents that sent him to college and to Europe for training.
Mr. McArthur:	He was the mill manager. He was also the son of the owner of the Irish mill owner.
Jane McArthur:	McArthur's daughter. She and David had a long, on-again off-again relationship.
Minnie Adams	She was a spinner in the mill who reads tea leaves and lived in the "castle".
Mr. Dan Lyttle	David's father who was very stern. He wanted his son to succeed and find a life beyond the mill, but struggled to understand when David finds a different path. He was put out of work because the Dye house operations were moved to the Aniston, Alabama mill. This loss of purpose eventually led to his early death.
Mrs. Lyttle	She too worked in the mill, but only until she was married. Once married, Mr. Lyttle insisted that she stay home. At her husband's death she had to return to work. She was proud to be a twister.
Mackenzie	The mill superintendent. He was a boyhood friend of Dan Lyttle back in the old country. Though he was not always liked, he did

	always help the Lyttle family by getting them work in the mill.
Blanchard	Dave Lyttle's musical mentor. It was his early interest that led Dave to pursue a career of singing.
Tim Murphy	He was Dave's age and had a desire to become a priest, but when his father's health fails, Tim had to go to work in the mill to keep the family going. Tim became an organizer of the Union movement in the mill.
Pete Knight	He was a little older than Dave and became a doctor in town.
Leona Knight	She supported her brother, Pete, through medical school and was a great support to both Dave Lyttle and Tim Murphy.

Some images from the book with strong parallels to Greenwich:

o   The men in the story went off to work carrying dinner-pails filled with thick sandwiches, cheese, and a banana.

o   The women workers were dressed in shawls pulled over their heads

o   The stream of workers on their way to the mill consisted of old men and old women, young men and young women, and boys and girls.

o   The Irish often wondered if they would ever get to see the old country again. It was their hope and dream to one day see the old friends.

o   Christmas parties put on by the mill in the old country were something to remember, and the custom had all but died out here.

o   Certain workers were recruited to help set up operations here, to bring their expertise.

o   Young men and women were often separated by an ocean waiting until enough money could be put together to allow both passage.

o   Baths occurred for everyone on Saturday night, after the week's work and in time for church on Sunday. Baths were done in a washtub.

o   A good man was one who worked to keep his family's needs supplied.

o   It was important to keep up the insurance so that you would not be a burden to those who would bury you.

o   A dollar for the bank, because savings were very important, was seen as a great birthday present.

o   Dinner was served at noon and supper was served at night for the mill workers, while dinner was served in the evening for the mill's management.

o   At the corner store a bill or account could be run and paid when money was coming in.

o   There was terror in life when the mill was closed or on reduced work; the result would be empty coal bins, unpaid interest on the mortgage, and mounting food bills.

o   Those who wanted a union in the mill were seen by many as   trouble makers.

o   There are good times and bad, but no family ever starved.

o   The union meeting was in Odd Fellows Hall.

o   The union lead to a 10 per cent raise.

o   The Castle was a tenement house. Those who lived there never got enough together to purchase their own home. The building itself was scary - never to be passed at night.

This is a great novel because it so closely parallels the story of the Dunbarton. Care should be taken, however, not to take the analogy too far. Five O'Clock Whistle is fiction and should be handled as such. It is very good reading for anyone interested in how a mill like the Dunbarton affects the lives of all who live in a small town.

Chapter IV - Tragedy

The Death of Agnes Devine - the First Tragedy

The Dunbarton's work force would see many tragedies throughout the Dunbarton's history. The people who came here were filled with hope and at times that hope was shattered when one of their number was taken through tragic death. Agnes Devine was the mother of nine children ranging in age from six weeks to twenty years. She and her family left Gilford on the 9th of Aug 1880 to come to Greenwich to work in the Dunbarton. They lived in the McMaster Block on Bleeker Street.

The events leading to her tragic death began on the 13th of Sept 1881 when Agnes had a kerosene lamp explode all over her. The kerosene soaked her clothing and caused it to catch fire. Her first instinct was to help her sleeping 6 week old child. Her husband, John, got to the child in time to save it. He was able to get his wife outside into the street where her older children Elizabeth and William attempted to put out the flames with their hands. Both William and Elizabeth were badly burned in this process. Finally Agnes's burning clothes were removed from her and she was taken back inside after their next door neighbor, John McCann, was able to put out the fire inside the home.

Agnes was attended by a Dr. Whitcomb who did what was possible to reduce her pain but her burns were too severe to allow her recovery. She was burned on the face, neck and arms and lived in agony until death came to her relief just past midnight on the night of the 14th of Sept 1881.

John Devine expressed his thanks in the Journal to all his friends and neighbors for their kindness and assistance in alleviating the suffering of his wife.

Unfortunately this tragedy was not over with the death of Agnes. The Devine's baby who was rescued from the fire died a month and a half later of membranous croup.

Attempted Suicide

A couple of the people associated with the Dunbarton attempted suicide:

James Mulligan   James was more generally known as the "Champion of Belfast". In April of 1886 he attempted suicide by throwing himself in front of an oncoming train. This he did in the switch yard in Greenwich and was rescued by one of the workmen who was repairing the track in the yard.

David Tomlinson   On 7 May 1913 David shot himself in the head and cried out. His sister Sarah found him and summoned Dr. Rogers. The wound was taped and Tomlinson was taken to the hospital by train. Miraculously he survived the gun shot and lived out the next 16 years with a .22 caliber bullet in his brain.

The Loss of the Little Child

The Batten Kill always had a luring effect on children of the village of Greenwich. All the kids in town used to swim in this river or just go exploring along its bank. Before the town established "the Beach" there were many popular places to swim. Indian Rock on the Easton side of the river above the first dam, the pier just below the Dunbarton (the pier was actually the remains of the foot bridge built by W. J. Wilson across the Batten Kill - see William J. Wilson and the Westwood Park on page 140), and the eddy also just below the Dunbarton dam. Unfortunately this lure often took its toll - the life of a child. These four children lost their lives to the river. In their death, the whole mill community mourned and gathered around the family in support. To each there is a story:

Phillip Henderson

Joseph and Roanna Henderson had three children: May F. Henderson, Phillip Henderson, and Agnes Eliza Henderson. On July 5, 1899 - when Phillip was just nine years old, he and his little sister Agnes waded across the Batten Kill below the Dunbarton mill dam in order to get some berries on the other side. Once Phillip had his fill of berrying, he noticed another boy, Charles Linendoll, was fishing from the dam. The river was so low that its entire volume was being used by the mill. Phillip joined the other lad until his sister called for Phillip. Phillip started to run along the dam and lost his footing and fell down the apron of the dam and fell into a pool of water about four feet deep.
Rather than help Phillip or call to the mill for help Charles ran home to tell his own mother. His mother told Mrs. Merrit Hill who told Roanna Henderson. Roanna Henderson quickly got on her bicycle and rode to the mill. Another boy had been sent to the mill to notify Joseph Henderson. By the time that Roanna arrived Joseph and a dozen men were out of the mill to the place where Phillip fell in. He was pulled from the river by John Richardson, Jr. Every attempt was made to revive Phillip while Joseph and Roanna watched despairingly. Dr. Whitcome was brought to the scene but he too was unable to revive Phillip. Sadly Phillip's body was wrapped in a blanket and sent home.

Apparently Phillip was a lovable young boy. He was a good singer and violin player. He was also an exceptionally bright child.

The loss of Phillip for Joseph and Roanna had to be a great one, the kind of loss that is every parent's worse nightmare. A loss such as this could easily have caused a great loss of faith. But that did not happen. Joseph and Roanna continued their active role in the church, community, and the mill.

Ronnie Hoffman

Ronnie was the son of Mr. and Mrs. Frank Hoffman. Ronnie, who was almost 8, went fishing off Indian Rock on August 17, 1943 with his brother Kenneth, 11 and Kenneth DeRagan, 10. Apparently Ronnie slipped off the rock and when Kenneth DeRagan noticed Ronnie in the water, DeRagan went in after him. Young DeRagan was able to get Ronnie to the surface but was unable to pull him to the edge of the river.

Kenneth Hoffman then went to his parent's (Mr. and Mrs. Frank Hoffman) home on Washington St and quickly a team of people were on hand to help, including Dr. Rogers, George Hill and Fire Chief Myers. Robert Patrick was able to pull Ronnie in with his row boat but efforts to revive Ronnie failed.

Ronnie was apparently a happy child and had made friends with many of the older residents of the town.

John Kelly

John was the three year old son of Mr. and Mrs. John Kelly. On Monday 21 Apr 1941, little John failed to return for supper. He was last seen about 5:30 pm playing on the east side of the Batten Kill just above the Bridge St. bridge.

Mr. Kelly began a search of the village stopping at every home where he thought the child might be found. As time passed, fear set in that perhaps little John had fallen into the river. By 8:30 pm the fire chief, Ralph Meyers, was contacted for assistance. Spot lights were obtained from New York Power and Light and boats were placed in the water but the child's body was not found. A large number of people assisted in the search which was abandoned at 2 am.

This was just the beginning of a four day search which ended Friday morning, April 24, 1941. John's body was found by Frank Lewis in an eddy 200 feet below the Mill Hollow dam (the second dam in Greenwich, New York). From scars found on the boy's body, it was determined that he must have hit his head on rocks when he fell into the river.

Daniel O'Hanlon

Daniel was the son of John and Mary A. O'Hanlon. Daniel was swimming in the Batten Kill just below the Dunbarton mill dam at what is called the Eddy on July 29, 1933. He apparently dove into the water and never came up. Friends he was bathing with (William Skiff and Isaac Jackson) pulled him from the water and brought him ashore. After a two hour resuscitation attempt by New York Power and Light employees, Daniel was declared dead. Daniel was 16 years old and had just graduated from junior high school in Greenwich.

Five Over the Dam

Perhaps the most devastating tragedy to befall the people of the Dunbarton happened after work on July 11, 1992. Apparently five of the mill's workers decided to borrow a row boat and cross the river for some berries. Sisters Ellen Jane and Frances Emerson, Sisters Jane Lowery and Mrs. Mary Pollock and Richard P. Richardson took the small row boat just after work at 6 pm apparently even before going for their evening meal. The party left shore somewhere above the Dunbarton mill dam. Ellen Emerson was given the oars and the party was on its way. Unfortunately the speed of the river exceeded Ellen's ability to row and soon the party was headed straight for the dam. When the boat got close to the dam Ellen apparently dropped the oars and fainted. Richard attempted unsuccessfully to get to the oars before it was too late. But he was too late.

The boat went over the dam with its five passengers screaming for help. Upon hearing the screams, Mr. McDonald came to help and was able to pull Mrs. Pollock from the river. Richardson was able to get himself ashore. Ellen, Frances and Jane were not so lucky. It was not till the afternoon of the next day that the bodies of these three were found in the Batten Kill near Middle Falls. In order to find the bodies a great number of people from the community came forward and helped in the search.

Both Mary Pollock and Richard gave accounts of the incident which were reported in the Journal. In Mary's account she thanks Mr. McDonald for saving her life. Mary's granddaughter Mary (Lesson) Brown was told this story as a young girl. She indicated that no one in her family was ever to go near the Batten Kill.

Chapter V - The Mill Itself

A layout of the grounds and Improvements along the way

From the moment that Hugh Dunbar McMaster purchased the mill property, the Dunbarton was in a state of being re-modeled. McMaster quickly had a structure built for flax storage and the flume installed for the water raceway.

When operations first began, the mill consisted of six buildings: a store house, a boiler house, a finishing thread shop, dye house, forge house, and of course the main mill. The main mill was 100 by 55 ft in length with three stories plus a basement. Initially the hackling and preparing was done in the basement while spinning, twisting and reeling were done on the first and second floors. The mill was heated by steam coils from the boiler house. The flume took the water underground and under the main mill to the waterwheel. From the tail of the wheel the raceway ran through the dye house where fresh water from the Batten Kill could be used to wash the yarn after it was dyed in the dye house. In these tight quarters, the Dunbarton still was able to employ about 120 people. Wm H. Tefft, editor of the Whitehall Chronicle commented in 1880 that the Dunbarton was contemplating the installation of a gas mill to manufacture gas for gas lighting. It does not appear that this was done and the lighting for the mill was done with kerosene until the installation of electric lights.

Sanborn Maps of the Dunbarton

The Sanborn Map company made several maps of the Dunbarton mill over the years. The first was drawn on a survey taken in 1884 and the last survey done in 1950. Sanborn made these maps along with similar maps of other businesses in Greenwich. The purpose of these maps was to allow interested parties to various aspects of businesses. For example, insurance companies would use Sanborn maps such as these to determine the risk of fire in establishing an insurance rate. They show interesting details such as what processes were handled on what level of the mill. They also indicate what types of fire protection existed. These maps show quite a progression of the extend of change to the buildings and grounds:

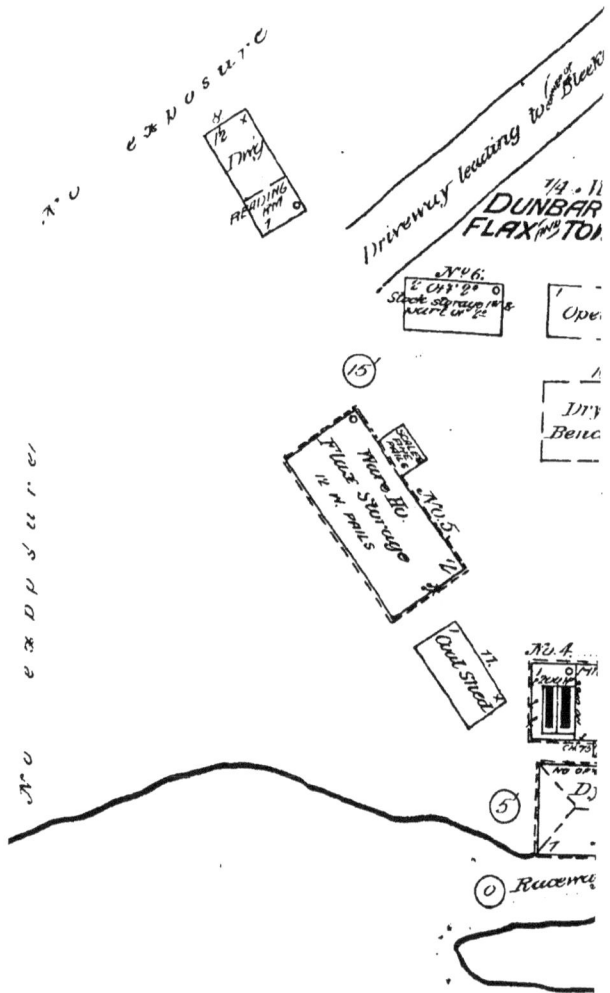

Ballen Kill Creek

The Dunbarton Mill as drawn by the Sanborn Map &

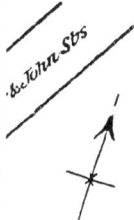

le S. W. or P.O.
ON MILLS. DUNBAR. MC.MASTER&CO.
SPINNING, LINEN THREAD AND TWINE M'F'G.
150 HANDS. WATER POWER. FIRE PUMP
CAPAC 200 GALL'S A MINUTE. 500' 2½"
LINEN HOSE. 50 BUCKETS DISTRIBUTED
THROUGH FAC. HEAT; STEAM. FUEL; COAL.
LIGHTS; KEROSENE LAMPS. NO ARTIFICIAL
LIGHT ALLOWED IN N°. 5 & 7. NIGHT WATCHMAN
WITH IMHAUSER CLOCK

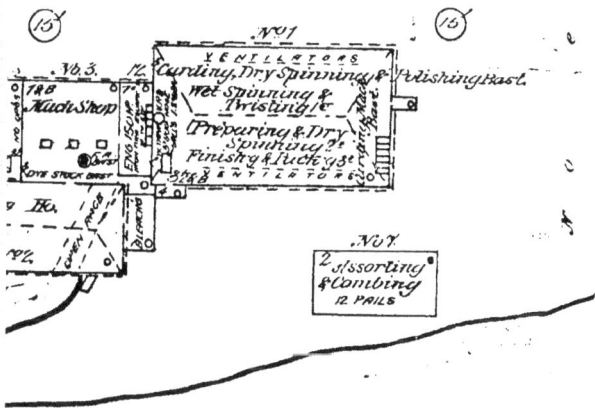

Dry Shed

No 3.

No 1

Curding, Dry Spinning & Polishing &c.
Wet Spinning & Twisting &c.
Preparing & Dry Spinning &
Finishy & Twce &c

No 2.
2 Assorting & Combing
12 PAILS

Publishing Company in 1884 reprinted with permission

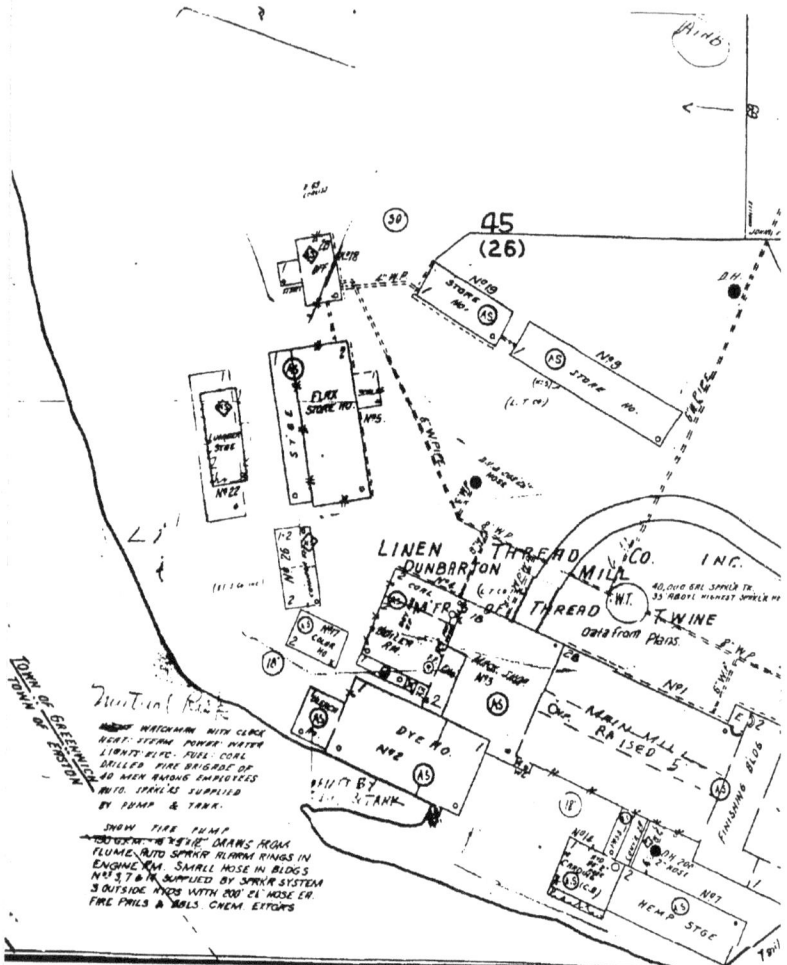

The Dunbarton mill as drawn by the Sanborn Map & Publishing Company

Map
Year   Description from map

1884   There were twelve buildings which constituted the mill. The main mill
        building was three stories with carding, dry spinning, wet spinning and
        twisting on the first floor. Preparing and dry spinning were on the second
        floor while finishing and packaging were located on the third floor. The
        sorting and combing (hackling) shop was separate. The dye house,
        machine, engine and boiler structures were additions to the main structure.

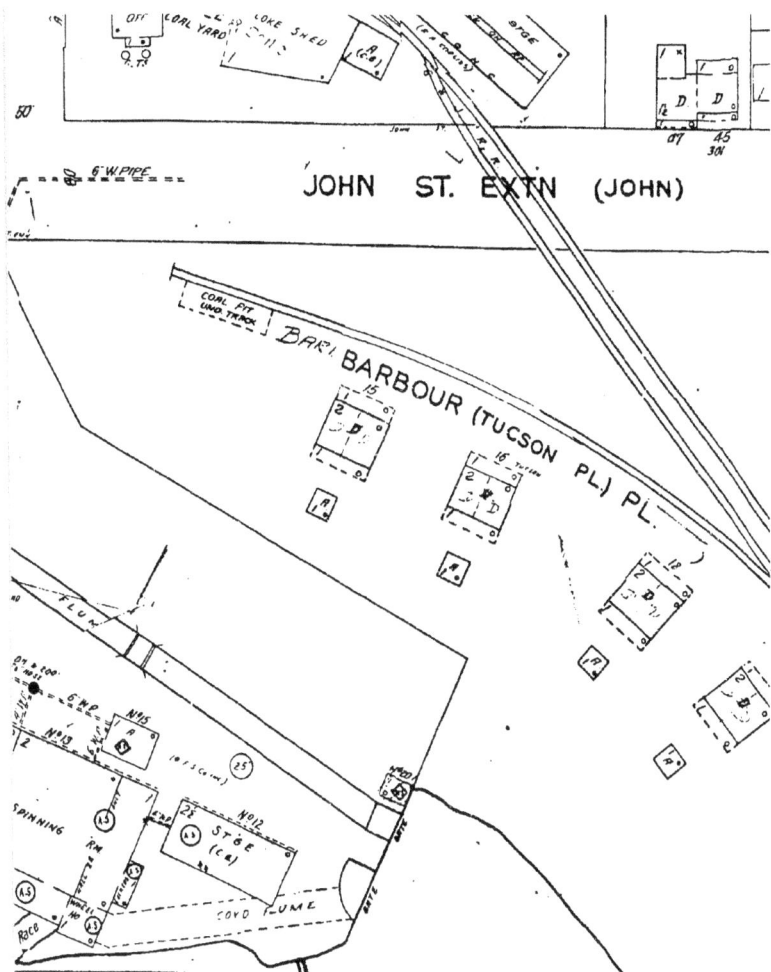

in 1950 reprinted with permission

The mill office was located in the second story dwelling which was also used for stock storage. The story and a half building, which was part of the original farm, was used as a reading room. There were several buildings for drying, coal storage and flax storage. In 1884, the heating was by steam and the lighting was by kerosene lamps and artificial lighting was prohibited in certain buildings. A 200 gallon per minute fire pump along with 50 pails for water was included in the description. The watchman was equipped with an imhauser clock.

1891   There were at this time sixteen structures to support the mill's operations. The flax storage building had been enlarged and had weighing scales added. A finishing shop was built and two storage buildings were completed. By this date the maps clearly indicate that lighting was done by electricity and a sprinkler system had been installed.

1898   From 1891 to 1898 an ash house next to the coal shed was the only addition. Two of the storage sheds are clearly labeled for flax waste and flax tow.

1907   At this time there were twenty structures on the mill property. Notable additions included a separate two story office, a two and a half story thread storage building, an oil house and a large new storage building. The mill was also supplied with a 6" water main from the village water system. This drawing indicated a second gate for the second flume and associated water turbine. The spinning building built in 1899 was inaccurately drawn as a store house.

1913   With twenty-three structures, major changes had been made to the Dunbarton, including the establishment of a separate spinning room building complete with an additional covered flume to support a second water wheel This map also clearly showed the row of ten apartments known as the Belfast Block. The night watchman was equipped with an eco magneto clock and made hourly rounds. Two types of sprinklers were indicated in the mill. A dry system for the storage areas and a water system throughout the remainder of the mill. The employees were drilled in fire brigade practices.

1925   In 1925 there were 24 structures associated with the mill with just the addition an oil shed. The fire brigade included 40 trained men. The most significant change on the map was the establishment of 5 double houses. These houses were along a street called Tucson Pl (a name I have only seen on these maps). Each was two stories and included front and back porches.

1941   By 1941 five buildings were removed from the property including three store houses and the oil shed and oil house. The oil buildings were built on top of the mill's covered flume. The map indicates covered flume was replaced by an open race way. The five double houses are now located on a street called Barbour Place.

1950   The mill shows little structural change in 1950 from the survey done in 1941.

Improvements Noted in the Journal

The Journal was very good about reporting on the improvements to the Dunbarton mill. The following are a few examples:

Date	Description of improvement
1880	The mill erected a flax store house, a dye house, a boiler house, a general store house, and thread finishing shop. The McMaster row house was built by Messrs. Whipple & Almy. A wooden flume was installed to carry the water from the Dam underground to the waterwheel inside the mill. The cost of this flume was reported to be $3,000 and was constructed by L. Land of Cohoes, New York. The flume was more than 450 feet in length and more than 128,000 feet of hemlock wood and 4500 lbs of nails and spikes were used in its construction. The water wheel in place was initially designed to deliver 130 horse power. The Dunbarton erected a high fence around its mill property.
14 Apr 1881	Dunbar, McMaster & Co. negotiated with Messrs. Whipple & Almy for the erection of ten more tenement houses to be built over the summer.
1 Nov 1883	The Dunbar, McMaster & Co. had one of the twenty telephones installed in Greenwich.
Jul 1887	The mill was closed for a week for repairs allowing the workers to enjoy the Fourth of July festivities.
Jan 1889	The Dunbarton closed on 24 Jan 1889 for three weeks for major repairs.
Oct 1890	Electric Lights were installed in the mill. Kerosene was used for lighting prior to this.
Jul 1891	The Dunbarton's truck team of horses donned a bright new harness and the wagon was freshly painted.
Mar 1895	A new spinning frame was received from Belfast. It was reportedly one of the largest and most improved in the US.
22 Sept 1895	A steam pipe which broke in the morning was repaired by afternoon and normal operations resumed.
March 1896	Work was slowed at the mill when some of the machinery connected with the waterwheel broke.

May 1896	The mill was closed for a short time to allow for the installation of a new waterwheel.
11 Nov 1897	The mill was shut Thursday night through Sunday to make extensive repairs to the boiler and the floors. (As a note, Ray Lang, who worked in the mill at a much later date, said that the floors in the Dunbarton were hardwood. If the floor were damaged for any reason, it would be repaired with a new piece of hardwood. In other words, when it came to maintenance, the Dunbarton did it right.)
19 Jan 1899	A new machine for the mill arrived and was put in place. It was hoped that the "new portion" of the mill would be complete by the 1st of March, allowing for up to 240 hands. This new building would house the "spinning" department.
11 Sept 1899	The Dunbarton Flax Spinning Company moved into its new office building. It was described as one of the finest offices in the vicinity of Greenwich. This fine brick building still stands today on the mill property.
5 Oct 1899	The Dunbarton announced its intention to build an additional building which would allow the addition of 40 more employees. The new building would be built with a concrete floor and brick walls. It was powered by an additional steam engine made possible by an already upgraded boiler.
May 1901	New equipment was installed in the Dunbarton. Repairs were made to the mill flume.
Nov 1901	A new dyeing machine was placed in the mill.
Jun 1902	Work was begun to blast rocks away from the Easton side of the Batten Kill to widen it. Work on a retaining wall was also begun.
Jan 1903	A second flume was installed to support an additional water turbine. This second turbine was 51 inches and was designed to drive the spinning mill which had been driven solely by steam power. In addition, the mill replaced the original mill wheel with a 54 inch turbine to drive the rest of the mill.
Oct 1904	Repairs and improvements to the Dye House were made.
Abt 1905	The Dunbarton was converted to turn out a few grades of thread as efficiently as possible. Prior to this time the mill produced many varieties of linen thread.

Sumr 1909	The old wooden and stone dam was replaced with a concrete dam.
Aug 1912	A chromatic whistle was installed to act as an alarm in case of fire. During a drill it was to sound an ordinary whistle while in the case of a real fire the whistle was to sound a scale and play "A Hot Time in the Old Town."
Fall of 1919	The tenement house known as the Belfast Block was split into five double houses. See "McMaster's Tenements" on page 125 for more information.
19 Dec 1919	The Dunbarton opened a nursery to care for the children of working women. See "The Day Care Center" on page 126 for more information.
Sumr 1923	One of the last major improvements to the mill was done during this summer. Ventilation pipes were installed in the preparing department. In this department many processes of doubling and drawing are performed to prepare the fiber for spinning. These processes create a large amount of dust and suction pipes were placed at points where dust was created. This allowed the workers to perform their duties with less dust.
	Many additional improvements were made at this time to consolidate departments and to improve overall efficiency. The size of the mill was not increased in any appreciable way. The Dunbarton was operating at full capacity which required improvements to be done while production continued.
	During this phase, the Dunbarton removed the bell from the belfry. See "The mill Had a Bell Before it Had a Whistle" on page 84.
Abt 1929	New and improved spinning frames were installed in the Dunbarton. This apparently played a roll in the decision of the Linen Thread Company to move some of its operations from the North Grafton, Massachusetts plant to the Dunbarton in 1931.
Aug 1932	A new flume was installed, replacing the original flume. The original was made of 2 by 8 inch lumber. These were laid edge wise to form a box of eight inches thick around all four sides. This flume was completely buried under ground and carried water from behind the dam to the water wheel within the mill proper. This flume served the mill from its start in 1880 to 1931 without concern. Eventually the wood did give way to a cave-in which led to the installation of a concrete flume. The new flume was deeper

than the original and was left open on top. It was reinforced by steel I-beams, was 400 feet in length and was spanned by several bridges throughout the mill yard. The mill went out for a two week vacation during this construction.

The Mill Dam

The original mill dam was built along with the original mill building in 1869 by the Greenwich Linen Company. This dam was built from lumber and stones and was to last for 40 years. During the spring freshet of 1909 a portion of the apron of the dam broke away. While efforts (which included the installation of flash boards) were underway to inspect and repair the damage, another major portion of the dam gave way 11 Jun 1909. This of course crippled the mill's water power and the Dunbarton was forced to generate all power from the 225 horse power steam plant. Still this was not enough power to run all departments at full capacity. The mill re-arranged schedules and the work to keep both plant and facility busy.

To rectify the situation, the Dunbarton decided to install a new dam. This time, a contract was let to have a concrete dam installed. Work began in July and was completed in October of the same year. This dam is still in place today.

Using water power as a major source of energy must have been a difficult task. The Batten Kill ranges from a raging stream to a slow trickle. The fall at the Dunbarton was one of about 8 feet - not a great drop - and therefore the power provided was completely dependent on the amount of water. Still the wise use of this resource was a benefit to the mill and significantly reduced the amount of steam power that was required to run the facility.

The Mill Had a Bell Before it Had a Whistle

Originally the mill had a bell that was used to mark time. This bell was installed in a belfry and was rung in the morning before work, at lunch and at quitting times. It was also the custom to ring the bell at 9 pm each night. This nine o'clock bell was called a curfew bell and told all the children in the west-end (the west-end refers to that part of Greenwich where most of the linen mill workers lived) that it was time to be home.

Sometime during the late 1910s or early 1920s a steam whistle was installed in the mill and this became the way in which time was marked. Isaac Jackson mentions the whistle in his notes on page 144 and Ramona Herdman titled her novel about a linen mill Five O'Clock Whistle. Even after the installation of the steam whistle, the practice of ringing the bell at 9pm continued until 1924.

On Thursday, Jul 12, 1924 the bell was taken down from the belfry as a part of a major remodeling of the Dunbarton. The bell made a few clangs on its way down as a way of protest and it remained silent for almost 20 years.

In April of 1942, the Linen Thread Company, at the direction of George Daisy, donated the bell to the Episcopal Church. The mill bell to this day is rung each Sunday by this church to call its members to worship.

It is interesting that the bell would end up in the Episcopal church. Many of the mill workers were of this faith (See "St. Paul's Episcopal Church" on page 121). The largest churches in Gilford are the Church of Ireland churches. The land for the Church of Ireland church was donated by the Dunbar, McMaster & Co. and there is an older church in Tullylish Parish about 1 mile from Gilford. John G. McMaster was a major contributor of his time and his resources to the Episcopal church while he was resident in Greenwich.

On Communicating With Gilford

Greenwich is some 7000 miles from Gilford, Ireland. Dunbar, McMaster & Co. would have had a difficult time keeping in synch if only mail service could be used. A letter sent from Greenwich to Ireland would require a 12 day voyage to cross the Atlantic. The return letter would have required the same amount of time. This rate of communication would have been fine for many business correspondence but some things require near immediate turnaround.

For immediate communications, trans-Atlantic telegraph was used. The first instance of its use was in January 1880 when Mr. Frazier of the Dunbar, McMaster & Co. of Greenwich received a telegram from Gilford, Ireland. This was the first telegram ever received in Greenwich utilizing the trans-Atlantic cable. Another instance of its use was in November 1881 when the Journal reported that a telegram was dispatched from the Dunbarton office by J. G. McMaster at 11:30 am. He received his reply at 5:05 pm! This was quite an accomplishment given that service included the time for the messages to be dispatched from the private offices to and from the telegraph office.

The Story of the Mill Property

In the early 1860's Arthur S. Pierce and his wife acquired land on both sides of the Batten Kill river. It was hoped that some industry might be established at the third fall in Greenwich. In the late 1860s a group of people formed the Greenwich Linen company. The reason that linen was chosen was because of the ready availability of flax. Washington and Rensselaer Counties were large producers of flax (See "Flax and Washington and Rensselaer Counties" on page 23). The Greenwich Linen Company were composed of Charles H. Cottrell of the Town of Greenwich, Adam Cottrell of the Town of Easton, William Weaver of Providence, RI and later

Greenwich, Horton Cottrell of the town of Easton, Henry P. Smith of the town of Greenwich, and Mary Cottrell of the town of Easton. These folks executed two purchases from Arthur S. Pierce to form a large enough block of property in Greenwich along the Batten Kill to establish a mill at the third fall:

Date	Seller	Buyer	Price/Property
5 Sept 1868	Arthur S. Pierce Sarah E. Pierce his wife	Charles H. Cottrell Henry P. Smith William Weaver Adam Cottrell Horton Cottrell Mary Cottrell	$10 plus mortgages of $1400 and $600/ 2 acres Easton Side of the Batten Kill
5 Sept 1868	Arthur S. Pierce Sarah E. Pierce his wife	Charles H. Cottrell Henry P. Smith William Weaver Adam Cottrell Horton Cottrell Mary Cottrell	$3000 / Property along the Greenwich side of the Batten Kill. Property subject to same mortgages of $1400 and $600 above.

Henry P. Smith was bought out shortly afterwards as follows:

Date	Seller	Buyer	Price/Property
8 Jan 1869	William Weaver Sarah Weaver, Wf Charles H. Cottrell Delia Cottrell, Wf Adam Cottrell Susan Cottrell, Wf Henry P. Smith Helen M Smith, Wf Horton Cottrell Mary Cottrell	Edwin Andrews	$1000 / Same property along the Greenwich side of Batten Kill as described in deed from Arthur S. Pierce. Sale subject to Mortgages of $1400 and $600 plus interest.
8 Jan 1869	Edwin Andrews	Charles Cottrell 1/4 Wm Weaver 1/4 Adam Cottrell 1/4 Horton Cottrell 1/8 Mary Cottrell 1/8	$1000 / Same property along the Greenwich side of the Batten Kill as described in deed from Arthur S.

			Pierce. Sale subject to Mortgages of $1400 and $600 plus interest.
1 Apr 1869	Hiram Corliss	Charles Cottrell 1/4 Wm Weaver 1/4 Adam Cottrell 1/4 Horton Cottrell 1/8 Mary Cottrell 1/8	$3000 / Property between Bleeker and Corliss Ave

Construction was begun to build a mill on this property. A large main building was erected along with a dam. Before operations could begin the company failed financially.

This gave rise to a family feud over who owned the property. Mary Cottrell brought suit against Horton Cottrell and Martha his wife, Adam Cottrell and Susan his wife, and Mary Cottrell, Betsey Cottrell, Terence Cottrell, Nathan Cottrell, John Cottrell, Walter Cottrell, and Grace Cottrell. The court appointed a referee, A. Dallas Wait, and ordered that the property be sold at public auction. The auction took place in Greenwich on 24 May 1877 and $12,000 was offered by Robert W. Lowbar, Trustee in the estate of Charles H. Cottrell. The deed was executed as follows:

Date	Seller	Buyer	Price/Property
10 Nov 1877	A. Dallas Wait, referee,	Robert W. Lowbar, trustee for the Estate of Charles H. Cottrell	$12,000/ Property, Buildings and contents, including waterwheel, shafting, pulleys, etc.

Robert W. Lowbar held the property in the estate of Charles H. Cottrell and made several attempts to sell the property. He found a buyer in Mr. W. N. Sprague who wished to use the mill to produce leather board. According to the People's Journal Mr. W. N. Sprague purchased the property. Several weeks later, however, the Journal indicated the Hugh Dunbar McMaster had purchased it although he had to offer $5000 to Mr. W. N. Sprague to get him to release his claim on the property. Apparently McMaster would only offer a premium of $2,500 to Sprague and it was through local subscription that the additional $2,500 was raised.

Since Hugh Dunbar McMaster was not a United States citizen, he was unable to purchase the property directly. He purchased the property through an agent as the following deed shows:

Date	Seller	Buyer	Price/Property
15 Dec 1879	Robt W. Lowbar, Trustee for the Estate of Charles H. Cottrell	John Stuart White, of 106 Worth St New York City	$6,650 / Property, Buildings and contents, including waterwheel, shafting, pulleys, etc.

John S. White is listed in Zell's United States Business Directory of 1881 as the sole agent for Dunbar, McMaster & Co. The work to set up the mill began before this deed was executed.

On April 30th 1881 the New York State legislature passed the following resolution:

AN ACT to enable Hugh Dunbar McMaster and others to take, hold and dispose of certain real estate in the county of Washington.

Passed April 20, 1881 by a two-thirds vote

The people of the State of New York, represented by Senate and Assembly, do enact as follows:

Section 1. Hugh Dunbar McMaster, John George McMaster, Percy Jocelyn McMaster of Ireland, now composing the firm Dunbar, McMaster & Co., are hereby authorized to take and hold as joint tenants and as such to convey and dispose of real estate in Washington county, state of New York, which they may now or shall hereafter require for flax spinning and the manufacturing of linen threads and linen fabrics, and buildings and appliances connected therewith, not exceeding one hundred acres, in the same manner as if they were citizens of the United States.

This bill was signed by the governor by 12 May 1881.

The Dunbar, McMaster & Co. then purchased the property as follows:

Date	Seller	Buyer	Price/Property
29 Sep 1881	John Stuart White of 106 Worth, New York City	Hugh Dunbar McMaster Percy Jocelyn McMaster John George McMaster of Gilford, Ireland now composing the firm of Dunbar McMaster and Company doing business at Greenwich as Joint Tenants	$6,650 / Property, Buildings and contents, including, waterwheel, shafting, pulleys, etc.

The Dunbar, McMaster & Co. started doing business under the name of the Dunbarton Flax Spinning Company in November of 1891. The Dunbarton Flax Spinning Company sold the property as follows:

Date	Seller	Buyer	Price/Property
14 May 1914	Dunbarton Flax Spinning Co	Barbour Flax Spinning Co	$100,000/ Property, Buildings, Water rights, engines, boilers, machinery, tools, etc. and all contracts, bills, good will, labels, etc.

In 1933 the Barbour Flax Spinning Company was dissolved and all of the property was conveyed to the Barbour Flax Spinning Company's parent company as follows:

Date	Seller	Buyer	Price/Property
15 Dec 1933	Barbour Flax Spinning Co.	The Linen Thread Co. Owner and holder of all issued and outstanding Capital Stock	$1.00 / Property and Buildings

The Linen Thread Company after announcing its intention to close operations sold the property as follows:

Date	Seller	Buyer	Price/Property
26 Sep 1952	The Linen Thread Co.	Sherman Wiesen, Inc.	$1.00 and other good and valuable consideration / Land, Buildings, and improvements.

Production Capacity

Very little information on how much was produced at the Dunbarton mill exists. When the mill first started production it was reported that the Dunbarton mills had 115 tons of flax, a quantity of hackled flax from Ireland, plus 23 tons of tow. Surely enough to get started.

It was also reported in June of 1880 that the mill would consume about 50 tons of flax per month or a car load and a half per week. The same article reported that the water wheel had the capacity for 130 horse power.

The People's Journal reported on 15 Sept 1897 the following figures about the Dunbarton:

4500	Twisting and Spinning Spindles
150	Horse power steam engine and boiler to support
100	Horse water wheel
up to 200	Operatives
600,000	Pounds of product per year

Meets and Bounds Description of the Property

Chapter VI - Working Conditions of the Mill

General Working Conditions

Working in the Dunbarton mill was difficult work. The processes involved in making linen thread are quite dusty. In the wet spinning room the temperature and humidity were very high to help keep the spinning process going well.

In the summer time the mill was very hot. There was no air conditioning to cool the rooms down. In the winter, the mill could get cold. Initially the mill was heated by steam coils only from the boiler room.

In spite of these difficult conditions, the Dunbarton's workforce really knew how to make the best of a difficult situation. Some workers were known to work a double shift when someone on second shift called in sick. Some workers stayed with the Dunbarton past the age of 70.

Work Hours

During the Dunbarton's first thirty-two years the mill operated on ten hour days, six days per week. In 1912 a fifty-four hour statute was passed which limited the number of hours that females could work to 54 hours per week or 9 hours per day. When this happened the Dunbarton arranged new hours for all operatives including the men to a new schedule. Although the Greenwich Journal is not clear, it appears that the Dunbarton adopted a 10 hour day for the five week days and a four hour day for Saturday.

In August of 1919 the hours were reduced to 50 hours per week. During the week work began at 7am and went till 5 pm with a one hour lunch break. On Saturday work was from 7am to 12 pm.

In the summer of 1931, the Dunbarton went to a two shift operation:

> Morning Shift: 6 am - 2 pm with ½ hour for lunch
> Afternoon Shift: 2 pm - 10 pm with ½ hour for supper

Pay

Very little is known about the pay received at the Dunbarton. George Daisy reported that when the mill first opened that men were paid one dollar per 10 hour day while women were paid 60 cents for the same 10 hour day. Children ages 11 and older were paid 25 cents per day as doffers. Overseers, hacklers, mechanics and skilled workers were paid on a higher scale.

It appears that in the early years of the mill, the people were paid by the hour. In September 1908 it was reported that a large number of operatives were being paid by the piece instead of by the day or hour. This change resulted in increased production. The Journal also reported that those on piece work were making several dollars more per week as a result.

During the spring of 1934 Greenwich held an "Industry Week" where industries and merchants put together displays to outline the products produced in Greenwich. The Dunbarton's exhibit was striking. Against a black background a single spool of linen thread was placed on a pedestal and labeled: "Irish Flax Sinew for lock stitch machines." There was also a sign which indicated: "This Nugget is Worth $100,000 per year to you" as a reference to the Dunbarton's payroll.

When the CIO union was established as the bargaining unit in the Dunbarton in 1937, a minimum wage of $15 per 40 hour week was established with time and a half for over time.

By 1942, the mill had established a custom of providing a week's paid vacation to its workers. This it did around the fourth of July each summer.

At the time the mill closed, the weekly payroll for the Dunbarton was about $5,000 for nearly 100 workers.

Number of Workers

We only have secondary sources as to the number of employees at the mill. The number of operatives working in the mill at any one time is not known. In fact the various sources are in conflict as to the number. The following are a few references:

15 Sept 1897   The Journal reported that the mill employed up to 200 operatives.

Mar 1899   Work was scheduled to complete an addition which would allow up to 225 operatives.

26 Jul 1939   The Journal reporting on a vote of the National Labor Relations Board on the independent union indicated that there were 93 non-supervisory non-office employees present for the vote.

May 1945   The Journal indicated that an 1880 payroll showed there were at that time 132 employees. This number was slightly higher than the 1945 number.

Jan 1951   The number of employees was reduced from 74 to about 50 when the mill went to a single shift from two shifts.

Child Labor

From its earliest days, the Dunbarton hired children to handle certain chores. Children began work in the Dunbarton at age thirteen. The most common task given to young children was doffing. Doffing involved the removal or "do offing" of the spools from a spinning or twisting frame under the direction of the spinner or twister. Doffers were also responsible to place new bobbins on the frame at the start of the spinning process.

The custom of children working at the Dunbarton was one brought from Ireland where children often began at an even younger age. In order to begin work at the Dunbarton, a child must have completed elementary school. The following is paraphrased from the compulsory education law which was in effect in 1906 (as printed in the Greenwich Journal):

> "No child has the right to be employed between the age of fourteen and sixteen years during hours of instruction (9 a. m. and 4 p. m.) between the first days of October and the following June, who does not at the time of such employment, present a certificate signed by the principal teacher of the school where the child has attended or other officer as the school authorities may designate, certifying that the child during the year preceding his application for certificate, has attended the public school not less than 180 days for that year, and having passed elementary studies required to be taught in such schools."

Child labor laws changed significantly throughout the years and this of course affected the age at which children could work at the Dunbarton.

The education of most of the children of the Dunbarton mill rarely went beyond the sixth grade. It was at this time the children were expected to become wage earners in support of the family. During the mill's first 50 years, only 25 of the Dunbarton mill worker's children were graduated from the Greenwich high school.

A custom in Ireland and continued in Greenwich was for the children to bring their entire pay home. This extra family income was given to the women of the house. She would then have the responsibility to make ends meet for the whole family. The child was given only a small portion back to spend as "their own" money.

Several people I interviewed mentioned this practice to me. In the early days money was a very hard thing to come by. There was just enough to pay the rent or mortgage, pay the grocer, pay for clothing, pay for heat, and save a little for one's old age.

Accidents and Safety

The Dunbarton, like most mills of its day, operated with machines throughout the plant, each getting its power from a main power shaft. The power was transferred via a heavy belt which could easily get caught in clothing. The equipment in the Dunbarton, especially the spinning equipment, operated at high speeds. There were rollers which took the flax fiber from one process to another. Given this environment, it would be easy to see that there might be many accidents along the way and indeed there were a few. However, the Dunbarton was incredibly free of serious accidents as the following known accidents would indicate:

A young boy   froze his hands while carrying the mail from the mill to the post office on Tuesday, 24 Jan 1882. According to Jane Whitaker this young boy was David Chambers.

John Hogan   had his fingers crushed in the machinery at the mill in April 1881.

James Corvin   was in the process of changing gears on a machine when the belt ran on. When this happened, three of his fingers were crushed. This happened 22 Mar 1883. Dr. Whitcomb attended.

Kitty Quinn   badly crushed her little finger by getting it caught in running machinery on 19 Dec 1885.

John Bailie   fell out a door on the second floor of the main mill building to the ground on 30 Aug 1893. He sustained some bruises and was attended by Dr. Whitcomb.

Benj. Babcock   fell from the scaffolding at the staging of a new building on 28 Nov 1898. Apparently Lewis Toronto, Jr. and Lewis Toronto, Sr. fell as well but only Benjamin was injured. Dr. Whitcomb attended to the injuries.

Peter Lowell   fell from a ladder on 11 Apr 1900 and badly fractured his arm. Dr. Mosher looked after the wound.

Wm Davison   suffered a severe injury to his hand at the mill 13 Jul 1900.

Jas. McLean   severely crushed his foot as he stood on a large gear of a machine that was suddenly started. His injury was on 6 May 1912. He was attended by Dr. Mosher.

Owen Murphy   On 18 Feb 1922 he was struck in the head by a heavy timber. A physician was called and several stitches were required to close the wound.

The Dunbarton participated in safety contests with 1800 other mills in New York State for a thirteen week period in 1930. The Dunbarton came through without a loss time accident and a score of 100% on their safety record with 43,968 man-hours. This ranked them tenth in their category.

Longevity - the Old Guard

It was quite common at the Dunbarton to have workers who had many years of service with the company. Not only did workers work until they were into their seventies, they also began work at a very young age. It was the custom in Ireland to begin working at age 12 and often children lied about their age to get into the mill sooner. In fact Thomas Wilson began working in Gilford at the wee age of 8 years.

THE OLD GUARD OF THE DUNBARTON MILL

Back: Thomas Wilson, Andrew Sallans, Patrick Smith, Thomas Emerson, Joseph Henderson. Front sitting: William Mulligan, William J. Tomlinson, Mary J. McAllister, Jane Chambers, Robert Meek. Very Front: William Reid

On 18 June 1919 the Greenwich Journal ran an article on the longevity of the mill's work force. At that time there were eleven employees who had an average tenure of about 52 years each and a total of 565 years among them. The Journal called them the "Old Guard". The article ran with a picture and included the following:

Name	Years of Employ		
Thomas Wilson	50	William J. Tomlinson	50
Andrew Sallans	58	Mary J. McAllister	45
Patrick Smith	50	Jane Chambers	53
Thomas Emerson	48	Robert Meek	52
J. J. Henderson	46	William Reid	54
William Mulligan	57		

This list did not include some 50 other employees whose years of service exceeded 20 years. The article was prompted when the Linen Thread Co. published a paper which boasted that eleven of its Paterson, New Jersey employees had an average of 42 years of experience. With this news Arthur Wilcox, the Dunbarton's general manager, decided to check the records. As you can see the "Old Guard" of the Dunbarton exceeded this by ten years on average! The Journal article also spoke very highly of the workers of the Dunbarton:

> "Another unique fact about this group of mill workers is that everyone of them is a tax payer in this village [in other words all were land owners], and some of them for considerable amounts. Nearly all live in their own homes and every one of them is a Liberty bond buyer, which speaks eloquently for the class of citizens the linen thread industry has brought to this community."

The article was re-run in the 14 Jun 1939 issue of the Greenwich Journal and at that time only Thomas Wilson and William J. Tomlinson were still living. In 1939 the Journal asked how much longer did each one work? Here's the Answer:

Thomas Wilson	retired in 1933 having passed his 72nd birthday. He came to Greenwich in 1887 as a hackler. He started in the Dunbar, McMaster & Co. mill in Gilford when he was about 8 years old. He worked for 64 years.
Andrew Sallans	retired about 1923 after 61 years of service. He came to Greenwich by way of Paterson, New Jersey After "retirement" he was a farmer.
Patrick Smith	left the Dunbarton sometime before 1925 when he was listed in the census as a state road worker.
Thomas Emerson	continued working in the Dunbarton until his death in 1928. He had accumulated 58 years of service. While a young man in the Dunbar, McMaster & Co. mill in Gilford, he lost an arm to a mill accident. He came to Greenwich with his family in 1880.
J. J. Henderson	"Dean of Dunbarton Workmen" retired on his seventy-fifth birthday in 1928. He was the first to arrive having worked for five years in Gilford. He attained more than 54 years of service.
William Mulligan	worked at the Dunbarton until his death in February of 1926. He gave 64 years of service. William came with his family in 1880 to Greenwich.
William J. Tomlinson	retired in July of 1930. He started when 12 years old in Gilford and came to the United States in 1882. He worked a total of forty-eight years in the Dye house in Greenwich and retired with 60 years with the company.

Mary J. McAllister	worked as a spinner in the mill until her death in March of 1928. When she died the mill was closed in her honor to allow fellow employees to attend her funeral. She came to Greenwich by way of Mechanicville, New York where she had also been a spinner. By calculation she worked 54 years, but the Journal indicated she had 48 years of service at the time of her death.
Jane Chambers	appears to have retired sometime before 1925 when in the census she is listed as doing housework. She came to Greenwich in 1881.
Robert Meek	received in March of 1927 a silver cup as the resident of the area who held a position with one concern for the longest period. At that time he had fifty-nine years and nine months of service. He began when twelve years old at the Dunbar, McMaster & Co. mill in Gilford. He had thirteen years of experience prior to coming to Greenwich to work in the Dunbarton here. He was one of the original immigrants to come in 1880. He retired in Aug 1930 with 63 years of service.
William Reid	continued his service until his retirement in about 1925 with 60 years of service. He came to Greenwich in 1884. On his retirement he took up a florist business.

Another Worker who had great longevity was:

| Mary Jane Richardson | retired after 60 years of service in Aug 1929. She began working in Gilford at the age of 9. Why she was not included in the list of the "Old Guard" is not known but she surely would have qualified! |

The above twelve individuals compiled a service record totaling at least 696 years with an average work life of 58 years!

Pensions were often provided to workers of such long service. When Mary J. Richardson retired she expressed thanks to the company:

> "...for their liberal policy in granting pensions to old employees."

Longevity - the Twenty-Five Year Club

In December of 1944 the employees of the Dunbarton mill established "The Twenty-Five Year Club" for those whose service to the Dunbarton exceeded twenty-five years. In May of 1945 the members were presented with a pin and a picture was taken of them as follows:

Front row:
Owen Murphy, Sr., 41 years, watchman; *G. D. Daisy, 26, Manager; *I. M. Flansburg, 30, Office Manager; *William Burns, 34, foreman; *Catherine McConnell, 43, winder; *James E. Ryan, 44, raw materials, union pres. and pres. of 25 Yr club; *George Jackson, 36, master mechanic; *Sam Crozier, Sr., 35, chief fireman; *James Cooke, 29, foreman; *James Wilson, 33, foreman; Sam Irons, 37, loft man

Second Row:
Elizabeth Kopa, 32, preparer; Lillian Gravlin, 26, winder; Mary McCann, 31, twister; P. J. McConnell, 36, assistant foreman; Mary Ann O'Hanlon, 40, spinner; James Doubleday, 35, mechanic; Robert Mahon, 27, wood-turner; Eliza Smith, 30, spinner; Rose Murphy, 27, spinner; Pearl Bowen, 26, reeler; Mary Ellen Boyle was a member in December 1944 but had died prior to the time the picture was taken in May 1945.

An * indicated continuous service years. These 21 employees had service totaling 698 years at the time of the picture. This is an average of 33 years per employee. Of the 21, twelve were born in Ireland and four were children of those who came from Ireland to work in the Dunbarton!

See the next page for a picture of the 25 year club.

The Twenty-Five Year Club - Photo taken in May 1944

Chapter VII - The Companies & Families

The Descent of Companies

The Dunbarton operated under several different company names. It is important to note however that the Dunbarton was known as the Dunbarton almost from the start, the earliest reference to this being May 1880. The progression from one company to the next took the following form:

A)   1879 - 1891 Dunbar, McMaster & Co. doing business in Greenwich, New York.

When Hugh Dunbar McMaster came to this country to purchase a linen mill he and his brothers were partners in the firm of Dunbar, McMaster, & Co. of Gilford, Ireland. In this partnership, Hugh Dunbar McMaster was the sole owner of all mill property in Gilford. With the Dunbarton, Hugh purchased this property with two brothers, John George McMaster and Percy Jocelyn McMaster.

Sometime in 1886 Hugh Dunbar McMaster formed a limited partnership called The Dunbar, McMaster & Co. Ltd. and all the Gilford mill property was deeded to the limited partnership under certain covenants.

B)   1891 - 1914 Dunbarton Flax Spinning Company

On the 26 of November 1891 the Dunbarton Flax Spinning Company was incorporated under the Laws of the State of New Jersey. All Dunbarton mill property was passed to this corporation.

On June 2, 1892 the <u>People's Journal</u> listed the following as incorporators:

H. Dunbar McMaster of Gilford, Ire, President
George Bingley Luke of Gilford, Ire[1]
James W. Wallace of Greenwich, New York, Vice President and Treasurer
J. Coleman Drayton of Bernardsville, New Jersey
Robert J. Wait of New York City, Secretary
J. McLean Nash of New York City

---

[1]George was the managing director of the Dunbar McMaster & Co. mill in Gilford. After the merger with the Linen Thread Company. George headed up marketing operations and his son William Luke eventually was the president of The Linen Thread Company, Ltd.

Hugh Dunbar McMaster clearly retained control of this mill and was President of the corporation in 1895 and 1896 as reported on the annual reports for those years. James Wallace of Greenwich is also listed as a board of directors member and secretary of the corporation.

In early 1901 Hugh Dunbar McMaster joined forces with the Barbours of Hilden, Ireland and became a part of the Linen Thread Company, Ltd. This same limited partnership was in control of the Linen Thread Company, Inc. in the United States. The "American" Linen Thread was in control of The Barbour Brothers and the Barbour Flax Spinning Company of Paterson, New Jersey. Some time around 1901 the control of the Dunbarton Flax Spinning Company passed to the Linen Thread Company, Inc. Although the exact time is not known, the Greenwich Journal announced on the 24th of April 1901:

> W. A. Barbour of Paterson, New Jersey and J. Davies of Newark, New Jersey, directors of the Linen Thread company, were in town Tuesday. They inspected the Dunbarton Linen thread factory here.

And again in September 1901 the Greenwich Journal indicated that officers of the Linen Thread Company held a satisfactory inspection of Dunbarton mill. Also on the 20th of Nov 1901 the Greenwich Journal reported that Arthur Wilcox was in Paterson, New Jersey on business of the Dunbarton Flax Spinning company. By 1909 William Barbour (who was then president of the Linen Thread Co.) was president of the Dunbarton Flax Spinning Company.

C)   1914 - 1933 Barbour Flax Spinning Company

On 14th of May 1914 the Barbour Flax Spinning Company purchased the Dunbarton Flax Spinning Company for $100,000. On the 15th of May the Dunbarton Flax Spinning Company was dissolved by unanimous consent of the stockholders.

D)   1933 - 1952 The Linen Thread Company, Inc.

On 15th of Dec 1933 the Barbour Flax Spinning Company, having been dissolved on 30th of Sept 1933 and also being that the Linen Thread Company was the sole owner of all outstanding capital stock of the Barbour Flax Spinning Company, the Linen Thread Company purchased the Barbour Flax Spinning Company for $1. The Dunbarton mill operated as a subsidiary of the Linen Thread Company, Inc. until the mill was closed in 1952.

Northern Ireland and Linen

Throughout the 18th and 19th centuries Ulster province in northern Ireland became the linen capital of the world. Prior to 1700 Ireland was like most countries in Europe. The women spun flax into thread and the men wove the thread into cloth. The linen that was produced was made only for local consumption. The quality of Irish linen was no better than that of other nations. So how did Ulster become so dominant in the production of linen? Most writers agree that this did not happen of its own accord but came about as a result of several key factors:

1) Ulster province was "planted" by many Scottish people during the early to middle 1600s. These people brought with them spinning and weaving expertise.

2) In 1696 the Parliament passed an act which allowed hemp, flax, linen, and linen yarn to be exported from Ireland into England without duty. At the same time laws were passed which placed a high tax on wool exported from Ireland to England. This law may have had religious overtones as it seems that Protestant England wanted to encourage the Protestant linen trade and to discourage Catholic woollen production.

3) In 1699, a large group of French Huguenots (Protestants) who were fleeing persecution in France settled near Lisburn. This group was led by Louis Crommelin and was supported by funds from the Irish Government. The group brought with them the art of making fine linens.

4) London provided a steadily increasing demand for linen.

5) Linen produced in Ireland was cheaper because rents and food were less expensive in Ireland than in England.

Throughout the 1700s linen was produced in the homes of small farmers. The women and children would be responsible for spinning and winding the thread while the men would be responsible for weaving the cloth. Often the family would take in a weaver to increase their output and income. The cloth, called brown linen, was then sold by weavers at local fairs and brown linen markets to linen-drapers who would bleach the linen white. Bleaching in those days was a complex process of washing in seaweed and allowing the sun to whiten, or bleach, the fabric. This white linen was then taken to Dublin where it was sold to the English merchants in the linen hall. In the late 1700s a white linen hall was also established in Belfast.

This basic form of linen production and distribution continued until the introduction of wet spinning machines in about 1825. For the next twenty years after 1825 spinning mills were established throughout Northern Ireland. Both the Dunbar, McMaster & Co. mill in Gilford and the William Barbour & Sons mill in Hilden were built during this time. No longer was it economical for woman to stay home and spin thread as it could be done cheaper in the mill and the thread was as fine in quality. This shift from homespun yarn to that spun in the mill also brought about a major change in the way weavers worked. A new system called the "put out" system developed. The thread mills would provide the weavers with thread on the condition that they would weave it into cloth. Once the cloth was completed it would be returned to the mill for payment.

This putting out system remained in place until the famine reduced the population through death and emigration to such an extent that there were not enough weavers. This lead to the establishment of large factories in Ireland which implemented weaving on power looms. The American Civil War also had a very significant impact on the increase of looms because the demand for linen rose dramatically due to the scarcity of cotton.

The Dunbar Family

Hugh Dunbar was baptized on 23 Jan 1789 in the Old Meeting House Green, near Banbridge, County Down, Ireland. Hugh Dunbar was engaged in the manufacturing of brown linen at Huntly Glen near Banbridge, when in 1835 he and two partners decided to establish a large scale linen thread mill. He and his partners were able to acquire 56 acres including the Corn mill and Tuck mill at Gilford, Ireland. The grant of this land and mills was subject to an annual rent of £325. In 1837 Hugh Dunbar was joined in partnership with John W. McMaster and two years later he was joined by James Dickenson. The firm Dunbar, McMaster & Co. was set up for the spinning of flax and the production of linen thread while Dunbar & Dickenson focused on the production of brown linen. The spinning mills at Gilford finally were opened with great fanfare in November 1841. It was reported that upwards of 800 sat down to tea to celebrate the opening of the mill.

The main mill building of the Dunbar, McMaster & Co., Gilford, Ireland

While Hugh Dunbar took on partners in the business he maintained ownership of the property rights. Hugh did not marry and on the 17th of April 1847 he died leaving his property to his four sisters. By amicable agreement two sisters, Ann and Jane

Dunbar, took control of their brother's business and property. Ann took her brother's position in the partnership of Dunbar and Dickenson and Jane joined the Dunbar, McMaster & Co. in 1854. Jane continued in the partnership until 3 Nov 1865 when she sold the family's share in the business to John W. McMaster (See the McMaster Family on page 105).

Hugh was very active in the community and his church. The Dunbars were members of the Presbyterian Church in Banbridge. He was ordained an elder in the church 6 Apr 1823. When the decision to build a larger church was made, Hugh Dunbar was asked to lay the corner stone in 1844.

What Hugh Dunbar is most remembered for, though, is his concern for the poor. It is said that he had 'the most lively sympathy for the sufferings of the poor, and set almost no bounds to his exertions to raise funds and make provisions for their wants'. It is believed that at the time of his death he was personally looking after the needs of 400 paupers in the Banbridge District. The Dunbar, McMaster & Co. provided schools and sites for the Presbyterian and Catholic Churches in Gilford. Hugh Dunbar is said to have died while passing out alms to the poor. It is said that he was found dead with a coin in his hand that he was about to give to a pauper.

Jane Dunbar proved to be very effective in the management of the firm. She too was known for her philanthropic deeds. She set up a trust to support the establishment of a school. The one stipulation of the trust was that the school must be "non-sectarian in character and be managed that all denominations of Christians can participate therein on equal terms." Jane was the surviving member of the Dunbar family and she died on 27 Mar 1874 at the age of 88 years.

The McMaster Family

John Walsh McMaster of Armagh joined in partnership with Hugh Dunbar about 1837. It was this partnership that established the firm of Dunbar, McMaster & Co. and also set up the great linen thread mill at Gilford. John W. McMaster remained in partnership with the Dunbar family until 1865 when he bought out the interests of the Dunbar family. This purchase included the entire rights to the mill property including the buildings and workers' houses.

Dunbarton House, Gilford, Ireland. The home of John Welsh McMaster and later the home of his son, Hugh Dunbar McMaster. This home was used as a military hospital during both world wars. It is now occupied by Dr. Alec Lyons

There was a tremendous boom in the linen industry during the early 1860s - about the time of the American Civil War. During this time John W. McMaster and his partners became very wealthy men. In 1866 he moved to dissolve his partnership with the Dickenson brothers. This dissolution lead to a famous law suit over the use of the Dunbar Dickenson and Dunbar McMaster trade marks. These trade marks provided the owner a ready market as the goods stamped with these marks commanded a considerable amount of money over similar goods. The Lord Chancellor of Ireland ruled in favor of McMaster in May of 1866, but his decision was overturned by the Court of Appeal in Jun 1867 which gave the trade marks to the Dickenson family. McMaster carried his case to the British House of Commons who overturned the Court of Appeals and it is said the workers in Gilford lit bonfires showing their support of the McMaster claim.

John Walsh McMaster died 11 Jul 1872 at Dunbarton House, Gilford and he left twelve children. Through his will he left all his property to his son Hugh Dunbar McMaster. Hugh Dunbar McMaster had been named for the founder of Dunbar, McMaster & Co., Hugh Dunbar.

Hugh Dunbar McMaster carried on a very successful linen trade after his father's death. His success can be seen by his willingness to expand the operation to the United States. The driving force behind this move was a very large import tax on linen thread. Prior to the establishment of the Greenwich mill, Dunbar, McMaster & Co. exported its products to the United States though various partners including William Spotten and James Douglas of New York City, New York. The Barbour

---

family were very substantial linen producers located at Hilden, Ireland. They had been successful in producing linen thread in the United States through the efforts of two brothers, Thomas and Robert Barbour. So Hugh Dunbar McMaster set out to follow their lead.

In late September 1879 Hugh Dunbar traveled to Greenwich, New York. He decided that the linen mill there would be perfect for his use. He purchased the property and began the process of setting up operations there in October 1879. Once he was satisfied with the progress he left the direction of the project to his brother John George McMaster. Hugh Dunbar McMaster purchased this mill property in partnership with his brothers John George and Percy Jocelyn McMaster. This mill was called the Dunbarton mill. John G. McMaster remained in Greenwich until April 1888 having purchased a home on Academy St. He then returned to Ireland where he died in 9 October 1889 at Gilford House. Percy of Gilford House, died 2 Dec 1887 at St. Anne's Heath Virginia Water, County Surrey.

In 1891 Hugh Dunbar McMaster set the Dunbarton mill up as a incorporated company called the Dunbarton Flax Spinning Company. It was incorporated 26 Nov 1891 according to the laws of the State of New Jersey. The people of Greenwich were well acquainted with H. D. McMaster because he made annual visits to the Dunbarton from 1879 to 1900. On one occasion he held a public meeting to describe a world tour he had completed. The proceeds of this meeting were donated to St. Paul's Episcopal church. In 1901 Hugh Dunbar McMaster joined the linen combine which was controlled by the Barbours of Hilden. On 29 Jul 1907 Hugh Dunbar McMaster died.

It is clear that the industrious efforts of two families (Dunbar and McMaster) lead to the establishment of a large linen mill in Gilford and then the establishment of the Dunbarton mill in Greenwich.

Awards of the Dunbar, McMaster & Co.

The Dunbar, McMaster & Co. carried a proud tradition of producing fine linen thread. It received medals of excellence for its threads in the following years:

> 1865 at Dublin
> 1876 at the United States centennial in Philadelphia, Pennsylvania
> 1882 at London
> 1883 at Cork
> 1884 at Toronto

Drawing of the Gilford, Ireland mill which may have been the one referenced in the People's Journal 25 Feb 1885

DUNBAR McMASTER & CO LTD
GILFORD MILLS, IRELAND

The Dunbar, McMaster & Co. gave a promotional calendar to the <u>Journal</u> office in February 1885. The calendar included a facsimile of the above medals along with a picture of the Dunbar, McMaster & Co. thread works in Gilford.

The Barbours of Hilden, Ireland and Paterson, New Jersey

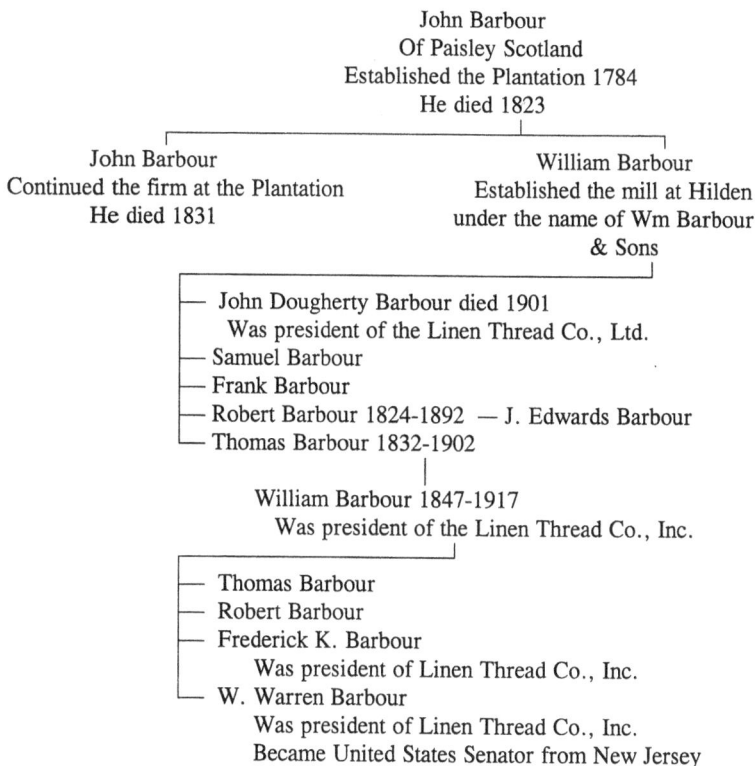

John Barbour
Of Paisley Scotland
Established the Plantation 1784
He died 1823

John Barbour
Continued the firm at the Plantation
He died 1831

William Barbour
Established the mill at Hilden
under the name of Wm Barbour
& Sons

— John Dougherty Barbour died 1901
 Was president of the Linen Thread Co., Ltd.
— Samuel Barbour
— Frank Barbour
— Robert Barbour 1824-1892 — J. Edwards Barbour
— Thomas Barbour 1832-1902

William Barbour 1847-1917
 Was president of the Linen Thread Co., Inc.

— Thomas Barbour
— Robert Barbour
— Frederick K. Barbour
 Was president of Linen Thread Co., Inc.
— W. Warren Barbour
 Was president of Linen Thread Co., Inc.
 Became United States Senator from New Jersey

To discuss the Barbours of Paterson it is first necessary to look at the Barbours of Hilden, Northern Ireland.

The Darbour family story begins with John Barbour of Paisley Scotland. He was involved in the linen thread business in Scotland and decided to move his business to Ireland in 1784. John is often credited as the one who introduced the first permanent manufacturing of linen thread on a large scale in Ulster. Prior to this time linen thread was spun only on a small scale and mostly as a cottage industry.

He established a linen thread village called the Plantation, near Lisburn. John built special homes for his workers at the Plantation which included a special room for the twisting machines. The Plantation also had warehouses for packing and dispatch.

John had two sons William and John who continued in the business after the death of their father in 1823. William separated from his brother and established a mill at Hilden also near Lisburn. He did this to take advantage of water power which was not available at the Plantation. Upon John's (son of John) death in 1831 William purchased the Plantation and consolidated all the operations at Hilden. To this day, linen thread is produced at Hilden.

William Barbour had five sons: John Dougherty, Samuel, Frank, Robert and Thomas. Each of these sons he brought into partnership under the name of William Barbour and Sons.

Sons John Dougherty, Samuel and Frank Barbour remained in Ireland and continued the Irish branch of the firm. By 1880 John D. Barbour was the sole son living in Ireland and he became the principle owner and director of William Barbour and Sons. It was his dream that linen thread firms should work cooperatively instead of in competition to improve the business. Based on this dream the Linen Thread Company was established (see "The Linen Thread Company" on page 111).

Sons Robert and Thomas came to the United States in the mid 1800s to help set up sales operations here for their father's concern. In 1864 Thomas and Robert Barbour established the firm of Barbour Brothers and purchased a mill in Paterson, New Jersey. In 1865 the Barbour Flax Spinning Company was formed with Thomas as president of the firm. The company began producing linen thread using imported machinery. This proved to be a very profitable adventure. Indeed, Robert and Thomas became so wealthy that they were said to be the largest tax payers in all of Paterson.

Thomas Barbour was president of Barbour Brothers until 1875 when he became vice-president and Robert became president. Thomas held this position until his death in 1892 and Robert held the position of president of Barbour Brothers until his death in 1902. Robert was succeeded by his son J. Edwards Barbour as president of the Barbour Flax Spinning Company until November 1909 when J. Edwards Barbour sold out his interests to other Barbours. He then managed the operation of a flax thread mill in Allentown, Pennsylvania and also established a flax thread mill at Paterson, near Lake View, New Jersey.

Towards the end of the 19th century the Linen Thread Company was established to accomplish a merger of many linen thread manufacturing concerns (see The Linen Thread Company" on page 111). Thomas' son William became the president of the American branch of this concern. As president William was a man of great influence. In addition to the Linen Thread Company, he was president of the Algonquin Co., the American Net and Twine Co., The U. S. Twine and Net Co., the Dunbarton Flax Spinning Co., the Dundee Water Power and Land Co., the Finlayson Flax Spinning Co., the Hamilton Trust Co., the Passaic Water Co., the W. & J. Knox Net and Twine Co., and the U. S. Twine and Net Co. He was also director of numerous other companies. During World War I he was given an honorary military title of colonel. William Barbour died 1 March 1917 in his automobile. The Dunbarton closed out of respect on the day of his funeral.

William Barbour had four sons: Thomas who was a professor at Harvard, Robert who was in charge of manufacturing at Paterson, William Warren who succeeded as president of the Linen Thread Company and later became a US Senator and Frederick Krup Barbour who became president of the Linen Thread company sometime after William Warren became a Senator. Frederick was the last of the American Barbours to be head of the Linen Thread Company, Inc. in the United States.

The Linen Thread Company

John Dougherty Barbour of Hilden, Ireland was driven by the vision that a unification of forces with other linen thread manufacturers would be of benefit to all. In this way, cut-throat pricing which only led to lost profits could be eliminated. To accomplish this task Mr. Barbour formed the Linen Thread Company, Ltd. This parent company was a holding company for the various concerns that would become a part of this combine. As a holding company the Linen Thread Company allowed each firm to continue as before except both the purchasing and sales departments were combined. In this way competition for raw material and for customers was eliminated. The first unification occurred sometime in 1897. In that year, The Barbour Brothers Co. (the sales wing of the Barbour Flax Spinning Company) was represented by Ben Bartlett at 110 Franklin, Chicago. In 1898 the firm was listed as the Linen Thread Company also at 108 and 110 Franklin, Chicago.

The firms that joined the Linen Thread were as follows:

William Barbour & Sons, Ltd., Hilden	This firm was the Irish branch of the Barbour manufacturing. It was under the control of John Dougherty Barbour at the time of consolidation.
The Barbour Flax Spinning Company, Paterson, New Jersey	This firm was established in 1865 by brothers Thomas and Robert Barbour for the spinning of Flax into Linen Thread.
The Barbour Brothers of New York	This firm was also established by Thomas and Robert Barbour for the selling and importing of linen goods.

The Marshall and Co. of Newark, New Jersey	This firm was represented by George A. Clark and Brother of Newark, New Jersey in <u>Zell's United States Business Directory for 1881</u> George A. Clark & Co. established extensive cotton manufacturing in Newark, New Jersey. Marshall & Co. was dissolved by unanimous consent on 26 Sept 1912 and merged into the Barbour Flax Spinning Company.
W. J. Knox, Ltd of Kilbirnie, Ayrshire, Scotland	The Knox family which controlled this firm began manufacturing linen thread as early as 1750. W & J Knox was consolidated with the Linen Thread Company in 1906.
Crawford Brothers of Beith, Ayrshire, Scotland	This family began manufacturing linen thread from at least 1775.
Finlayson-Bousfield & Co. Ltd, of Johnstone, Scotland and North Grafton, Massachusetts.	This firm was started in Glasgow and while still small it moved to Johnstone in 1844. The Finlayson-Bousfield mill was located on High St in Johnstone. There were many workers from Gilford who emigrated to Johnstone to work for this firm. In 1880 Finlayson-Bousfield established a mill at North Grafton, Massachusetts in the "Upper Mill" which had been built in 1826 by the New England Manufacturing Company. Finlayson-Bousfield also imported the principle labor to run this mill from Scotland and Ireland. The American branch was incorporated 10 Jul 1901 in New Jersey and the firm's name changed to the Finlayson Flax Spinning company. On 26 Sept 1912 the Finlayson Flax-Spinning Company was dissolved into the Barbour Flax Spinning Company. The mill in North Grafton closed in July of 1931 for tax and labor reasons and some of the work was shifted to a second shift in the Dunbarton mill. The Nolan and Kopa families moved to Greenwich from North Grafton at this time.
Ainsworth & Co. of Cleator Moore, Cumberland	In the 1882 <u>New York State Business Directory and Gazetteer</u> this firm was represented by T. Ainsworth of 60 Church St (Cleator Mills, England)

Dunbar, McMaster & Co. Ltd., of Gilford and the Dunbarton Flax Spinning Co. of Greenwich, New York	Firm founded by Hugh Dunbar and others in 1836. Greenwich mill established in 1879. Joined the Linen Thread early 1901.
F. W. Hayes & Co., Ltd, of Seapatrick	Firm established by Frederick W. Hayes at Seapatrick, County Down, Ireland. Banbridge is in the Parish of Seapatrick.

Early in the 20th century the Linen Thread Company also acquired the following firms through purchase:

Robert Stewart and Sons, Ltd of Lisburn	Robert Stewart built his first mill in 1836 and took his sons Robert and James Andrew as partners in 1845. In 1889 the mill was rebuilt.
Lindsay Thompson & Co. Ltd of Belfast.	This firm was established in 1882 by an old Tyrone County family by the name of Lindsay. They established the firm using Prospect Mill built in 1868 by John Savage in Belfast.

Whatever Happened to the Linen Thread Company?

When the Dunbarton mill closed in 1952, the Linen Thread Company, Inc. in the United States had mills in Paterson, New Jersey, Newark, New Jersey, Salem, Oregon, Kearny, New Jersey, Gloucester, Massachusetts, Baltimore, Maryland, and Blue Mountain [Anniston], Alabama. The Linen Thread Company, Inc. was a wholly owned subsidiary of The Linen Thread Company, Ltd. which was then headquartered in Glasgow, Scotland. In January of 1959, Indian Head Mills, a cotton textile producer agreed to purchase the Linen Thread Company, Inc. for $12 million. At the time, the Linen Thread Company, Inc. was headquartered in New York City and had 3000 employees.

During the 1960s the Linen Thread Company, Inc. was operated as a subsidiary of Indian Head Mills, Inc. Also during the 1960s the Linen Thread headquarters was moved from New York City to Blue Mountain, Alabama and the mills of Paterson were closed. Employment in the Linen Thread Company, Inc. decreased to about 1000. 22 May 1962 the Linen Thread Company was formally merged into Indian Head Mills, Inc. By 1970 the Linen Thread Company was part of a group of companies known as the Specialty Textiles Group of Indian Head Mills, Inc.

In 1973 Thyssen-Bornemisza, a privately held Dutch company, purchased an equity interest in Indian Head Industries. In 1974 Thyssen-Bornemisza purchased 90% of Indian Head stock.

In September 1975 Hanson Industries, Inc., a subsidiary of Hanson Trust Company, Ltd of Great Britain, completed a $35 million purchase of Indian Head's Specialty Textile Group. This purchase included what was left of the Linen Thread Company of Blue Mountain, Alabama. The textile group was organized into the Carisbrook Industries.

The only mill remaining at Blue Mountain, Alabama continued operation as Blue Mountain Industries, a Carisbrook/Hanson Company.

The mill at Blue Mountain, Alabama continues to make linen thread which is essentially the same as the shoe thread produced in the Dunbarton. The primary application for this thread is in the shoe repair trade. They produce this thread from rove which is spun in Great Britain or Hungary. Currently this thread sells for about $17.50 per pound. Blue Mountain Industries continues to hold the Barbour Trade Mark for the United States which consists of a single red hand (the same symbol as the red hand of Ulster).

Other United States Linen Manufacturing Concerns

At the time the Dunbarton mill was established there had been several other concerns in the United States that had produced linen on a large scale. By 1882, all had abandoned the manufacturing of linen. One of the main reasons for abandoning linen was the difficulty in procuring quality flax for the production of thread. Some companies who abandoned linen production:

o   The American Linen Company of Fall River, Massachusetts This concern was established in 1852 to handle the production of white linen starting with unhackled flax. At first its product was in such demand that they could not keep up production, but by 1858 the demand was so low that they converted their entire production to cotton.

o   The American Linen Thread Company of Mechanicville, New York. This company was established in 1852 and produced linen thread. It remained in operation until January of 1882 when it was purchased by a Boston based company. The Journal reported that the mill was going out of business, its equipment was being sold at public auction the 31st of Jan 1882. William Seaton, the Dunbarton's first superintendent came from this company. Thomas Doubleday also worked in this mill prior to coming to Greenwich.

o   The Willimantic Linen Company of Willimantic, Connecticut. As its name implies, this manufacturing concern was established for the production of linen thread but converted its entire production facilities to the manufacture of cotton thread in the 1850s. This they did when their foreign supply of flax dried up as a result of the Crimean war.

o   The US Linen Company
o   The Sprague Linen Company

Chapter VIII - On Religion and Faith

Catholic - Protestant

As most of the mill's labor force came from Northern Ireland it was natural that the workforce have a mixture of Catholic and Protestant workers. It was also natural that these people would bring with them many of the old ways of relating to one another. The mix of the mill's population can be seen from the following table:

Dunbarton Workforce Including Management

Year	Catholic	Protestant	Unknown
1880	6	29	19
1900	19	78	15
1910	33	52	19
1920	36	47	27

In the early years there were only a few Catholic workers. Over time this number grew both in real numbers and relative to the total working population. Management on the other hand remained primarily in the hands of Protestants as can be seen from the following table:

Dunbarton Management

Year	Catholic Managers/ Foremen	Protestant Managers/ Foremen	Unknown Managers/ Foremen
1880	0	3	0
1900	0	12	0
1910	1	7	0
1920	2	9	1

All of the mill's top managers (mill managers and superintendents) were Protestant. Only three of the mill's known foremen were Catholic.

As I gathered information from various sources, I found that there were many examples of religious tension. I record the following quotes as it relates to this topic:

"When we were young, you knew that you were different from them [the Catholics]. For example, if you were to walk down Hill Street we were told always to walk on the Protestant side of the street. You see the Presbyterian Church was on one side and the Catholic was on the other. To make our side even more 'Protestant' Joseph Henderson, the pillar of the Presbyterian Church, lived right across the street from the Catholic Church. As far as I knew the Catholic children were instructed to walk on their side of the street on Hill."

"The Irish were funny people. They could see in another person their best friend and their bitter enemy at the same time. And that was the way it was between the Catholic and Protestant."

"My sister married one of the Catholics as her first husband. She went slowly insane and we all knew it was on account of the fact she married one of them."

"We were told never to date a Catholic because they would make you raise the children Catholic."

"Never trust a harp [Catholic]."

"My Grandfather was Catholic when he came to Greenwich. One of the mill foreman invited my grandfather to church and suggested that they meet at the drug store before church. The two men met at the appointed time and to my Grandfather's surprise they went to the Presbyterian Church. He met my Grandmother that day in Church and they got married and he became a Presbyterian. His whole family disowned him and would have nothing to do with him. This break in the family continued until my Grandfather's sister died and then the family began to mend itself back together again."

"My mother was Catholic and my father Protestant. They buried my mom in the Catholic cemetery and the rest of my family is buried in the Protestant cemetery. It seems odd that my parents should be separated in this way."

"I was taught to hate the Catholics. This was the way I saw things until the war when I served right along side some Catholic men. We went through hell in the Pacific and that was where I discovered that Catholic or Protestant we are all just as vulnerable to bullets."

"I was so glad that we [Catholic and Protestant] got along. When I went back to Ireland, I couldn't believe how badly the two groups got on and how they were fighting. Here we are living next door to each other and life went on."

Joseph L. Shannon in his history of St. Joseph's Parish indicates that this prejudice while present was tempered:

> Despite an admirable degree of ecumenism and good will, the people of Greenwich, of whatever religious or political persuasion, were not immune from the prejudice, bias and bigotry which were endemic in this country. Apart from the adolescent fighting of school-boys based on whether they were from the "South End" or "West End" or "North Side," the division between Protestant and Catholic in Northern Ireland, based on economic and religious issues was much more serious and came with the immigrants from that area. Many who considered themselves native to the country felt threatened by the massive waves of immigrants. Many immigrants sensing their vulnerability resented what they deemed exploitation and disdain on the part of the majority. Political differences added spice to this struggle. Bitter as this division became at times, and subtle in its manifestations at others, Greenwich never indulged in the persecution and violence that characterized the Know-Nothing Movement in the mid-nineteenth century. A sense of Christian civility and good will has prevailed down the years in Greenwich.

During 1903, the village of Greenwich was involved with the question of liquor licensing and whether or not the village should go dry. A "taxpayer" wrote the Journal that the "new Catholic" church was being built on liquor money. Fr. Green, the Priest of St. Joseph's parish pointed out that there were some 18 establishments in the village with licence to sell spirits. Of these only seven were owned by Catholics!

There is little mention of an Orange Order (an Irish Protestant organization) branch being established in Greenwich. There was an ad for an excursion sponsored by the Loyal Orange Institution of Troy, Albany and vicinity in the 26 Jun 1890 Journal. The ancient order of Hibernians was established in June of 1892, the organizers being Irish Catholics other than mill workers.

The Journal also held a different standard between Catholic and Protestant. The average length of a Protestant obituary was larger than those published for Catholics. It is not hard to guess - based solely on the length of the obituary - the religion of the person who died.

When it came to support the soldiers of world war I, the Knights of Columbus, a Catholic men's group, was even able to count many Protestant mill workers as supporters when they raised money in support of raising army camps.

There were many marriages of couples who shared different faith traditions:

Patrick Quinn and Catherine McAllister
William Bright and Anna McDonald
Robert Adamson and Elizabeth Toronto
James Mulligan and Elizabeth Shields
Joseph Lyttle and Sarah Donnelly
William McQuade and Lizzie Lowell
Patrick Murphy and Rachel Cooke
Robert Doubleday and Grace Clarke
Thomas Doubleday and Maria Wilkenson
Isaac Chambers and Stella Aiken

St. Joseph's Parish

St. Joseph's Catholic church has its roots as early as 1833 when it was reported that there was a priest living in Greenwich. This report however was not well substantiated and it really was not until 24 Jan 1869 that the priest of St. Patrick's church in Cambridge, Fr. Waldron came to hold mass at Temperance Hall in Greenwich. There were apparently as many as 250 attending. On that day there were two girls ages 19 and 17 who had never even seen a priest. A Sunday school was also established with ninety children enrolled. This was a very large turnout indeed, and it was clearly apparent that a church should be established at Greenwich. On 2 Jul 1869 the <u>Washington County Post</u> announced that a group had been formed to establish the location of a church in Greenwich. Just two weeks later the same paper announced that the corner of Bleeker and Hill streets had been procured for the purpose of establishing a church there. The property consisted of two lots and the lots were purchased for a sum of $1,500. Interestingly the lot was owned by members of the Methodist church building committee and had been purchased as a possible site for the "new" Methodist church. During the spring of 1870, the young catholic mission purchased the Methodist's frame church and had the building moved to the corner of Hill and Bleeker streets. This frame building was built in 1839 by the Methodists and was replaced by a brick structure completed in 1870. The first baptism in St. Joseph's church was recorded 31 Jul 1870.

This mission was quite active and set about the work of establishing themselves in the community of Greenwich. The parish was for its first 11 years a mission of St. Patrick's church in Cambridge. In the spring of 1879, the congregation felt itself strong enough to establish themselves as a parish in their own right. The congregation committed to funding a salary for a priest and to establish a residence for the priest. It is interesting to note that many of the 104 signers of this commitment letter were to work in the Dunbarton over the years. Names such a Dooley, Hogan, Dwyer, Curry, Millett, and Duffy are on this list.

The first resident pastor was Fr. Thomas Field and he arrived in August of 1879.

This was just one month before it was announced that H. Dunbar McMaster was to establish his linen mill in Greenwich. The infusion of the Irish workers for the Dunbarton no doubt played a roll in the up building and life of St. Joseph's parish.

St. Joseph's church prospered from 1879 through 1903 when work was begun to complete a large brick church building. The frame building was moved from the corner further up hill street and the ground was broken on 2 Jun 1903. It would take until 8 May 1910 until the church structure could be dedicated to the glory of God by the Rt. Rev. Thomas Burke, Bishop of Albany. To pay for this structure the local congregation held annual fairs and plays. These were much supported by the community of Greenwich.

Rev. R. Hardigan of Gilford, Ire preached in St. Joseph's church on 23 Jul 1882. It is interesting that Rev. Hardigan would take such an interest in the people who left Gilford and come and visit them in Greenwich.

When St. Joseph's moved in 1905 to connect their sewer line to a line that was installed to clear surface water on John Street, the Dunbarton went to the village board and protested. They were successful in blocking this action.

John J. McCann, the eldest son of John McCann, was ordained a priest 9 Jun 1906 in the Cathedral at Albany. John's father was a linen mill worker. Father McCann was ordained by Bishop Burke with a class of seven. Father McCann officiated at his first Mass in St. Joseph's church in Greenwich on Sunday 10 Jun 1906. The members of St. Joseph's presented the newly ordained priest a purse of about eighty dollars.

The list of those contributing to the Christmas and coal collections of the church in 1909 included 398 names. Of these at least 68 people were at one time or another associated with the Dunbarton.

The United Presbyterian Church

By arrangement of a committee headed by Rev. A. W. Morris, who was then pastor of the South Argyle Presbyterian Church, the United Presbyterians began holding weekly Sabbath services in the Greenwich Opera House on 28 March of 1880. This was the first "Presbyterian" worship service held in Greenwich.

On Monday night April 26, 1880 water was released down the new flume of the Dunbarton mill and the mill formally began to produce linen thread. On this very same night, a group met at the Greenwich Opera House to discuss the possibility of establishing a Presbyterian church in Greenwich. The conclusion of the meeting was to petition the Argyle Presbytery to organize just such a church.

On May 26, 1880, a commission appointed by the Argyle Presbytery received members into the new congregation by certificate. Of the first members admitted to the young congregation the following were associated with the mill:

James Wallace, Joseph Henderson, Mr. and Mrs. James McLean, Sarah Meek, and Sarah Wilkenson.

The United Presbyterians apparently made an offer to the Opera House to convert its building to a church for $5,000 in April 1881. This offer must not have been accepted, as the congregation then set about the work of having a church built. A site was selected on Hill Street for the new church.

On the 8th of May 1883, the United Presbyterian Church dedicated its new church building. To celebrate, the Rev. R. J. Cunningham of Shusan, New York and the Rev. A. W. Morris each preached a sermon to the young congregation. The building cost a total of $6,400 and at the dedication a total of $1,200 remained to be paid. The congregation contributed $850 and A. W. Morris was able to present a pledge of $350 from churches in western Pennsylvania. These totaled $1,200, the balance to be paid. The young congregation had a church fully paid for. The church building was constructed on Hill Street and was designed and supervised by Mr. George Almy. It was 65 x 35 feet and seated 450 people.

Men from the Dunbarton mill under the direction of Robert Hammel were responsible for the flagging (paving the sidewalk with slate flag stones) in May of 1884.

In March of 1897 the Journal published the committee members of the United Presbyterian Church. There were a total of 43, 21 of which were associated with the mill.:

Mrs. J. J. Henderson, Thomas Emerson, Sarah J. Reid, Maggie Redpath, Lillian Wallace, John Giffin, George Ruddock, Mrs. David Roberts, Minnie Ingraham, J. J. Henderson, Minnie Wilson, Robert Meek, William McQuaid, Anna Brown, Hugh Wallace, Mrs. Thomas Wilson, Sarah Meek, Valentine Ruddock, Minnie Reid, Rachel Redpath, and Mrs. Archie Weir

In 1967 the United Presbyterian Church merged with the Dutch Reformed Church in Greenwich to form the United Church of Greenwich. The United Church has an active congregation and is a member of the Presbytery of Albany.

St Paul's Episcopal Church

Utilizing the services of the pastor of the Schuylerville Episcopal Church, a group of people began the "Episcopalian Society" in Greenwich holding services as early as 1870. St. Paul's Episcopal Church was incorporated Sept 1, 1874. In 1880 it became clear that the influx of a large number of Protestant Irish workers meant that there would be a larger population of those interested in worshiping in an Episcopal setting. The largest population of the Dunbarton's Protestants were members of the Church of Ireland. The Church of Ireland was the Church of England in Ireland or the Episcopal church. Given this large new population, the vestry men set on the task of erecting a church building.

On 30 Apr 1880 the barn which stood on the Church's property was moved in preparation for the building of a church. In this year, Rev. Windsor came from Philadelphia to be pastor of this congregation. The Wardens and Vestrymen of the congregation in 1880 were all native to the United States. Within a year, the immigrated Irish influence was directly felt in the Episcopal church because John G. McMaster was elected as a warden while William C. Seaton and Robert Moles were elected vestrymen. In 1882 it was clear that the Irish immigrants from the Dunbarton were making a strong contribution to the life of this congregation. John G. McMaster, Andrew Sallans, and James Bright were elected as vestry men.

Unfortunately, just as the Dunbarton workers were making their mark on this congregation, the Reverend Windsor crossed ways with one of the church's members. Windsor racked up a $100 bill with a local merchant and vestrymen. This caused a major schism in the church, from which St. Paul's had a difficult recovery.

In December of 1882, St. Paul's opened the doors of its new church building. This building was designed and built by Whipple and Almy and was 35 x 85 feet. The building still stands on Main Street just east of Mowry park. The church included a tower of 80 feet. At its dedication the church was given a large and elegant Bible, hymnal and two prayer books from Reverend J. Harding of St. Paul's Church of Ireland Parish in Gilford. Many of the Dunbarton's workers were married or baptized by Reverend J. Harding.

The building itself was completed in 1884 at a cost of $5,425. The vestry men, rector and warden offered resolutions of thanks to H. D. McMaster and the Ladies Mite Society for their part in the building up of the Church. John G. McMaster gave half the money to purchase the Church's heating system. H. D. McMaster held a talk at the Odd Fellow's Hall on his travels, the proceeds of which went to help pay for the church building. In 1897, the parish was able to pay off the mortgage and the church building was consecrated.

The Episcopal church had many ups and downs and always the people of the Dunbarton played a part in the life of the congregation. According to the Reverend James Lowery, St. Paul's actually had to close its doors between 1888 and 1890 due to financial woes. During these early years many of the Church's members went elsewhere to assure regular attendance for themselves.

Apparently some sources of friction in the church were the use of candles, the introduction of a cross, the vesting of the choir and other external worship aids. This was troublesome for many of the Dunbarton's workers. Many saw the use of such things as popish or Catholic. This was something to be avoided at all cost by any Orange Irishman. It can be rightly said that St. Paul's was seen by the Irish as the church of the Orangemen. The following incident was captured by Reverend James Lowery:

> "The story is told of Bishop Nelson that he came down to visit a congregation full of Irishmen for confirmation. He was cornered by a bunch of Celtic complainants, who threatened to leave for the Presbyterians because their parson had been so "papist" as to put a cross on the Holy Table. The rejoinder settled the matter once and for all. "Gentlemen, you are in America now. If you wish to be American you must live with American ways."

Prior to this incident Orange Day, July 12th had been celebrated in St. Paul's. After this, the tradition of Orange Day celebrations came to an end.

In April 1942, the Linen Thread Company, at the direction of George Daisy, donated the bell to the Episcopal Church (See "The Mill Had a Bell Before it Had a Whistle" on page 84). The labor to install the bell in the church was also donated. The following is an excerpt from the April 28, 1942 vestry meeting:

> "The vestry wished to go on record as extending their thanks to Mr. George Daisy for the donation of the bell, Mr. Fulmer for making the standard and bearings and Mr. Silkworth was appointed chairman of a committee to supervise the installation of the bell."

The mill bell is to this day rung each Sunday by this church to call its members to worship.

Chapter IX - On Housing and Child Care

On Owning Your Own Home

The hope of home ownership was one of the calling cards for those who came from Ireland. One of the first of the Irish immigrants to purchase a lot and build a home was Joseph Henderson. He bought his lot on Hill street in April 1882, the year of his marriage to American born Roanna Higgins.

As a result of this desire to own one's own place there are many stories that relate to housing in Greenwich. One story is told that the mill's workers were promised land if they would come to the Greenwich to work. Some folks in Greenwich called the land on lower Bleeker, VanNess, Corliss, John and Washington streets the promised land. This was where most of the mill's workers lived. Still others called Gray Ave the promised land because none of them ever ended up there. From the record, it does not appear that the mill actually gave anyone land. The only purchases of property by the mill were for the mill itself and a home on Academy Street for the use of John G. McMaster.

What did happen, something that could never happen in Ireland, was that many of the mill's workers not only ended up owning their own homes but became considerable property owners and landlords themselves.

A look at the 1900 US census is instructive. There were a full 20 heads of household who were associated with the mill who owned their own home. Of these there were nine who owned the home free of mortgage. In this same year there were just 29 heads of household who were renting their home.

By 1910, of the head of households living in Greenwich who had come over from Ireland to work in the mill, 35 owned their own home, 12 of those free of mortgage, and 27 heads of house hold were renting.

In 1920, 29 head of households living Greenwich, who had come over to work in the mill owned their own home while 16 rented.

Greenwich Before and After the Dunbarton

A simple look at maps of Greenwich before 1880 reveals that lower Bleeker Street, Lower Hill Street, Lower Corliss Ave, Lower John Streets and John Street Extention and much of Washington Streets were just open fields. With the influx of linen mill workers there was a tremendous need for housing. These open fields provided the building room needed. Over time houses went up. Most homes were built with two families in mind. At times the design was for one family on one side and another family on the other. An Example of this is 23 & 24 Bleeker Street, the home at the corner of Bleeker Street and John Street. This home was once occupied by Sam Crozier, Sr. on one side and his brother Richard Crozier on the other.   William Reid's home on at 41 John St is another example of this style. Other homes were built with an idea of having an apartment upstairs. Many homes on Bleeker and Hill Street are built on this plan.

The approach of having two families occupy a home was quite good for the average linen mill working family. Often a family could afford to purchase such a home and help cover expenses by renting the other half of the home. As a side benefit to this, many of the mill's workers became landlords in addition to working in the mill.

McMaster's Tenement

At the corner of Washington and Bleeker Streets Dunbar, McMaster & Co. built a row of tenement houses. This row of ten apartments were built on a style like the row houses that were common in Gilford, Ireland. They consisted of two rooms downstairs and two rooms upstairs. This tenement was built in 1880 by Messrs. Whipple and Almy to help meet the immediate need for housing. Initially these were known as McMaster's tenement but later the row was referred to as the "Belfast Block".

In 1919, the mill decided to cut the row of apartments into five sections consisting of a double house each. A street was created called Barbour Place where the homes were placed. Each double home was cut away from the rest, moved and placed on its own foundation. A basement was added to the original two rooms up and two rooms down. A kitchen, pantry, toilet room and a vegetable closet were located in the basement. The homes were wired for electric lights, porches were added to each unit and a separate shed was built in back. In addition a coal furnace was installed for heating.   These double homes were in use by mill workers up until 1952 when the mill sold the property to Sherman Weisen, Inc.

The rent on the two family homes was very reasonable. Shirley (Garrett) Friday indicated that as Mr. Daisy's secretary she was once asked to go collect the rent. She recalled that rent was only 2 to 3 dollars per month!

The Castle

One of the largest apartment complexes in Greenwich was called the Castle. This building was located on John Street in what was recently the home of Coach George and Pat (Burkin) Jackson. This structure was complete with a tower and was quite a sight to behold. Many of the mill's workers would call the Castle home over the years. The building itself was around as early as 1883 when Edward Crossen caused a disturbance when he kicked out a tenant. The Castle posed quite a problem for the village over the years and was the source of many disturbances. On one occasion in 1947, the village threatened to close the place, having found chickens in the basement, porches in major disrepair, inadequate outhouses, open drains and numerous structural problems with the building. The owner, Victor Kenyon made a commitment to clean the place up.

19 Corliss Ave

Perhaps one of the best examples of Victorian architecture in Greenwich is at 19 Corliss avenue. This home was built by James Wallace, the mill's managing director from 1888 to 1909. James built this home in about 1901. After James' death in 1909, his widow lived there for many years. The home eventually was sold to Jack Crozier the son of Samuel Crozier, one of the mill's workers.

The Superintendent's house

The house at the corner of Bleeker and Washington Street was where the mill's superintendent lived. This was indeed a convenient location, being just a block from the mill's main gate and just across the street from the mill's tenement houses. It was to this home that William Seaton first brought his family up from Mechanicville. When he left, James Bright took possession of this home.

The House on Washington Square

One of Greenwich's finest homes was located on Washington Square. This home still stands and is a great example of a Greek revival home. When the home came up for sale, Thomas Wilson was mulling over the idea of purchasing the home. When Thomas mentioned this to some of his working friends they said "That homes not for you Tom." "Its in the wrong part of town and beyond your means." Thomas proved them wrong and he purchased the home and lived out his years in it.

The Day Care Center

Even today, American business is not quite sure what to do about child care. It is a responsibility that business does not wish to accept.

When the Dunbarton was having difficulty attracting enough women to run its operations in Greenwich in 1919, the Dunbarton solved this problem by establishing a nursery. They built a two story structure at the corner of John Street Extension and Corliss Avenue on mill property especially for this purpose.

The mill provided this service while charging the women only a nominal fee. The fee apparently did not even cover the cost of the food that was provided three times per day to the children. A professional nurse, Miss Aldora VanderWerken of Troy, who had been in charge of a ward in a hospital in Rochester was hired. Mrs. Raymond Stevens acted as an assistant. Eight mothers took advantage of this service on the day that the nursery was opened, 15 Dec 1919, and it was expected that more would take advantage of the service at a later date.

At some point the nursery was converted to into a family residence. William George Jackson, the mill's master mechanic moved his family into this converted house. When the mill closed in 1952, the house was sold to Jackson, prior to selling the rest of the property.

Chapter X - War and the Dunbarton

The Spanish American War

The Spanish American War lasted only a very short time and impacted only a few workers from the Dunbarton mill. The following men connected with the Dunbarton in Greenwich played a part in the war effort:

James Devine   James enlisted in the army Co. H. 7th U. S. Infantry in Nov 1891 long before the war as a private. His rank quickly rose to corporal and then to sergeant. At the start of the Spanish American war he was sent to the front line where he served and was injured in the shoulder during one of the engagements. While returning after the war he was taken sick on board ship. He went to a hospital in Providence, Rhode Island. After some recovery he went to Montauk Point camp and finally to Fort Wayne hospital in Detroit, Michigan. When his company left Fort Wayne, James attempted to conceal his illness and go with them to Vancouver, Washington. Upon discovery of his illness he was sent back to Fort Wayne Hospital where he died in May of 1900. His body was returned to Greenwich for burial.

Tom Quinn   Thomas Quinn with Pierce R. Faddon, Joseph Delavergne and Frank Goodrich joined the army in late April 1898 soon after the war broke out. They joined the 32nd, Separate Company, F. L. Stevens captain, of Hoosick Falls. The four were sent off by a large crowd at the Greenwich & Johnsonville Depot on 29 Apr 1898. By mid June Thomas was sent to training camp in Tampa, Florida. From here he wrote many letters which were published in the Journal. In his letter of 7 Jun 1898 he indicated that he had found Jim Devine and had dinner with him and in his letter of 14 Jun 1898 he wrote that he had heard that James Devine was on a ship to Cuba. In his letters he whimsically complained about getting paid late and getting his picture taken. Life for him appeared to be a "hobo's life."

Thomas's view of life at war was to change very dramatically as the following letter, written on his return trip to Greenwich, published 17 Aug 1898, indicated:

"I want to tell you something that happened," he writes, " coming up on the train, the day we left our divisional hospital, a fellow was brought in, with his foot hanging off. They amputated his foot, and we could see everything. I was in the same car. He was unconscious most of the time. I had never seen anyone like that. There were four of us that got up every day and dressed, and we were made to take our turns watching him. He would try to get up and get out of bed. When we got to Atlanta, I was taking care of him. He was noisy then. The doctors gave him some morphine to quiet him. He tried to get up once after that and I laid him down. He was very quiet after that, and when I looked at him in about five minutes, he was dead. His mouth was wide open, as were his eyes. His teeth were as black as coal. I called the doctor, and he pronounced him dead. You can imagine how I felt. I went to bed, and was sick all night, and part of the next day. They buried the poor lad in Atlanta, the next day. I hope I will never see anything like that again."

World War I

The Dunbarton mill and its family of workers contributed heavily to the War effort. The following persons associated with the mill served during the war:

Joseph Adamson	Was the first person in Greenwich to join the war effort by returning to Ireland where he joined the British Army, 1st battalion, Royal Irish Fusiliers. He saw much service and was taken prisoner of war on March 31st, 1918. As a prisoner his prison was bombed by allied forces and he died in Hams, France, 6 Jun 1918.
Harry C. Boyle	Honored by the Catholic Daughters of America of St. Joseph's parish for service during World War I. He was the husband of Isabelle Fletcher.
John J. Boyle	Honored by the Catholic Daughters of America of St. Joseph's parish for service during World War I.
Robert Chambers	Drafted and returned home honorably when he failed his eye exam.
George Daisy	Was second Lieutenant, field artillery. According to Arthur Wilcox, George met several key people from the

Barbour Flax Spinning company while in the service and this is how he got his start with the Dunbarton.

Anthony Denaro	Honored by the Catholic Daughters of America of St. Joseph's parish for service during World War I.
Michael Denaro	Honored by the Catholic Daughters of America of St. Joseph's parish for service during World War I.
Robert Davidson	An enlisted man according to Journal list 9 Jan 1918.
William J. Fletcher	Was in a Machine gun company, 303rd Regt.
David Kinnen	Was a Battalion sergeant, 13th Inf. regular army
John Lyttle	Sold out his market to join the army in the summer of 1918. He was also the last soldier from Greenwich to return from Europe arriving in Greenwich in Nov 1919.
William Lyttle	Joined the army. While in training he got sick and died at Otisville, Maryland 5 Jan 1919.
Arthur McCann	Honored by the Catholic Daughters of America of St. Joseph's parish for service during World War I.
John J. McCann	Served as a Chaplin in the Army in France. Honored by the Catholic Daughters of America of St. Joseph's parish for service during World War I. He returned Jul 1919.
Thomas McCann	Honored by the Catholic Daughters of America of St. Joseph's parish for service during World War I.
Samuel McCune	Served in France and was discharged and returned home in April of 1919.
Thomas McCune	Served in Company M 111th Regt.
Joseph McGrouty	Served in Company M. 111th Regt.
John Millett	Wounded in the leg by shrapnel on 21 Oct 1918 in Argonne, France while fighting with the American forces there. He was taken to a hospital where he died three days later. Initially he was buried in France but his body was brought to Greenwich and buried with honors in July of 1921.

Lewis D. Quinn	Honored by the Catholic Daughters of America of St. Joseph's parish for service during World War I. Auto repair detachment, 1st expeditionary brigade.
Robert J. Quinn	Honored by the Catholic Daughters of America of St. Joseph's parish for service during World War I.
George Reid	Returned to Ireland at the outbreak of the war and enlisted in the Royal Dublin Fusiliers. He was decorated for conspicuous gallantry in battle.
Thomas Richardson	Served in the Navy. He wrote a letter about his life in the Navy, not to his parents but to Arthur Wilcox on 17 Jun 1917.
George Seed	Traveled from Greenwich to Albany to enlist in the British Army in 1918. Initially the Journal quoting an Albany newspaper indicated that George joined to seek revenge for lost relatives. The following week however, George's letter to his father gave his own thoughts: "to think of the lives of French and Belgian children, of English women and children and even of our own former Belfast neighbors, and then if he has any manhood his heart will respond to the cry for enlisted men."
Harold Simms	Was a member of the British Army who died from a shell explosion in France. He was William Simms' brother.
Patrick J. Smith	Honored by the Catholic Daughters of America of St. Joseph's parish for service during World War I.
Daniel Smyth	Was the son of Mr. and Mrs. John Smyth, a member of the North Belfast regiment U. V. F. He was killed on 7th July 1917 in France.
David Tomlinson	Served in the Navy
Frank Tomlinson	Was a member of Machine gun company 303d Regt.
William Tomlinson	Served in the Headquarters Regt. 2nd division
James Wilson	Served in France and was discharged and returned home in April of 1919.

Greenwich, like much of the rest of the country, celebrated the armistice twice. The first time occurred on Thursday November 7th when a premature announcement

---

through an incorrect dispatch indicated that the armistice had been signed. This first celebration caught the village by surprise. The news began with bells and mill whistles sounding to the news that the fighting had stopped. Apparently anyone who could walk left their home or place of work and proceeded to Washington Square where a parade around the town began. People grabbed flags and bells and horns and marched up and down main street. Those who had cars drove them and blew their horns. The village buses were filled with people of all ages. The excitement continued well into the evening. Even when news arrived that the war indeed was not over it was not enough to stop people from celebrating.

The second and real armistice was celebrated on Monday Nov 11, 1918. Festivities in Greenwich began early in the morning, before breakfast, with the ringing of bells and mill whistles. The day was passed in parades and marching,

After the war, the citizens of Greenwich placed plaques for each of those who died in the war effort. These plaques including ones for William Lyttle, John Millett and Joseph Adamson were originally placed near the Greenwich & Johnsonville Railroad Depot on Bleeker Street. At some point they were moved to Mowery park on Main Street where they remain to this day.

World War II

The Dunbarton mill and its family of workers contributed heavily to the war effort. In 1942, the workers of the Dunbarton gave up their traditional paid week vacation in order to keep production going. According to the journal a full 98 percent of the mill's workers were contributing to war bonds through payroll deduction. The following persons associated with the mill served during the war:

ARMY	Aaron A. Hand	Wm J. McQuade
	George Jackson	George R. Mulligan
Robt F. Adamson	John Jackson (gave life)	Gerald E. Nash
Raymond J. Burch	Isaac Jackson	William J. Nolan
William J. Burns	William Jackson	Felix O'Hanlon
David R. Chambers	Frank Kopa	Stephen O'Hanlon
Willis Chambers	John P. Kopa	William J. Quinn
Walter J. Couser	Joseph P. Kopa	Ken G. Richardson
John Crozier	William J. Lyttle, Jr.	Burdette W. Sallans
Richard J. Crozier	Edward L. McCann	Ralph H. Sallans
Samuel Crozier, Jr.	Thomas B. McLean	Albert F. Yandow
Jas. E. Doubleday	Allen McLean	Ray J. Yandow
Patrick E. Fletcher	Albert McQuade	
Arthur M. Gravlin	Kenneth McQuade	
Marine Corps	Wm L. Adamson	James Murphy

Navy

Herbert Adamson
Richard Crozier, Jr.
Norris Doubleday
John Fullerton, Jr.
Nicholas Karp

**Served but branch
unknown**

James J. Lesson
Christie E. Lyttle
Paul McQuade
Philip D. McQuade
Thomas McQuade
Francis C. Murphy
Raymond Murphy

William C. Boyle
Ted Doubleday
Jas. J. McReynolds

John J. Nolan
Samuel J. Nolan
Donald Perkins
Paul E. Quinn
Frank Richardson
Ralph Richardson
James E. Ryan, Jr.

Lewis D. Quinn
John F. Richardson
Joseph R. Wever

Chapter XI - Immigration & Irish Relationships

Immigration

During the first year of operation the Irish came in groups. The workers had been specifically recruited for the job of starting up operations in Greenwich. It is not known who paid the passage for these early workers. After the first year of operation, it was clearly the worker who paid for their own passage. The passage cost was significant and often required the help of established friends to make the passage possible.

In about 1880, Andrew McBrinn, a grocer located in Gilford, advertized that he was a general Emigration Agent.

Naturalization

As soon as the first group of workers had passed the statutory time for naturalization, most made the pledge to renounce the Queen of England and pledge allegiance to the United States. On 24 Oct 1885, the following workers were naturalized at Salem, New York:

William Bright	John Ewart	Robert Meek
Joseph Brown	Joseph Henderson	James Mulligan
Richard Kerr	William Heran	John Mulligan
Thomas Couser	Isaac Kinnen	Robert Mulligan
William J. Devine	James Little	William Mulligan
Thomas Emerson	Michael McDonald	Andrew Sallans

Others waited a few extra years. For example, James Bright, who arrived in 1880 did not become naturalized until 1888. James Wallace also one who came in 1880 took his pledge in 1890.

It is important to note that the laws during this time period were written so that when the male head of household was naturalized, his wife and minor children were also. Single females were never naturalized separately until the 1920s.

UNITED STATES AMERICA

DEPARTMENT OF STATE

To all to whom these presents shall come, Greeting:

I, the undersigned, Secretary of State of the United States of America, hereby request all whom it may concern to permit

Thomas Wilson

a Citizen of the United States

safely and freely to pass and in case of need to give

Description

Age 38 Years

Stature 5 Feet 11½ Inches Eng.

Nose straight

Mouth medium

Chin square

Hair reddish brown

Complexion fair

Face full

Given under my hand and the Seal of the Department of State, at the City of Washington, the ..... day of ..... in the year 1899, and of the Independence of the United States the one hundred and twenty third.

Signature of the Bearer

Thomas Wilson

Thomas Wilson's passport for his 1899 trip back to Ireland

Some Who Came and Returned

Not all mill workers came to the United Stated and remained. Many came for a few years and returned to Ireland. Others made various trips to Ireland and returned to Greenwich.

Here are a few examples:

George Reid   George came here about 1908 with his sisters Margaret and Elizabeth. He married Eva Mahon the sister of Robert Mahon and Tillie (Mahon) Mulligan. George and Eva had children in 1911 and 1913 and then Eva died. George became home sick and heart broken. He returned to Ireland, enlisted in the Royal Dublin Fusiliers during the first world war, and was decorated for conspicuous gallantry in battle.

Margaret Neill   Margaret lived in Belfast around 1907 when she made inquiries in newspapers for her lost brother Jack York. Jack had disappeared many years earlier. Margaret had two unmarried daughters living with her at the time. One day Jack appeared at her door and convinced her to go to America. She took her two daughters to Essex County, New York but not until the older one, Margaret, married Samuel Crozier. Samuel joined the family some weeks later once he had enough money to pay for his passage. The family moved from Essex county to Glens Falls, New York and then to Greenwich. Margaret Neill never really liked it in the United States. She said she wanted to die in Ireland. In about 1921, Margaret was taken back to Ireland by her daughter Margaret Crozier. On the trip Margaret Neill suffered a stroke. She died in Ireland, word being received by Margaret Crozier as she was returning to the USA.

Lizzie Miller   Lizzie was a spinner in the Mill. She was a cousin of Margaret Crozier and lived many years with the Crozier family. In 1932, a sister of Lizzie had a husband who died. The sister wrote Lizzie and asked that she return. Lizzie did return at that time.

James Bright   James was one of the first of the Irish to come to Greenwich arriving in 1880. James also took a five week visit to Ireland during the summer of 1899. He was superintendent of the mill from 1884 to 1901. He decided to go back to Ireland to pursue a business career there and took his family to Belfast in the spring of 1901. In August of 1903 he returned to Greenwich and resumed his duties at the Dunbarton.

Samuel Brown	He came from Belfast and assumed the position of superintendent in the spring of 1901 when James Bright went back to Ireland. In August of 1903 James Bright returned to his old position and Samuel Brown returned to Belfast.
Robert Forsythe	He came to Greenwich in the fall of 1889 to assume the position of bookkeeper for the Dunbarton. He unfortunately became ill with consumption. In hopes that a return to his family in Ireland would aid in the remission of the tuberculosis he went back to Ireland in late 1894. He died there on 25 April 1895.
John Giffen, Sarah Burns, Ellen O'Hanlon Kate O'Hanlon	John Giffin, Sarah Burns, Ellen and Kate O'Hanlon left for Ireland in April of 1900. John and Sarah were expected to return while Ellen and Kate were expected to stay in Ireland. In June 1900 John Giffin was the only one to return, Sarah, Ellen and Kate remained in Ireland.
James Wallace	James took several trips. His first trip back was in April 1885 when he took a two month vacation to see his parents. He sailed 5 Jul 1887 for Gilford on business of the Dunbar, McMaster & Co. He returned on Monday 1 Aug 1887. On June 6, 1902, sailing on the Celtic, Mr. and Mrs James Wallace and daughter Florence set sail for a two months tour of England, Ireland, Scotland and the continent.
Mary O'Hanlon	When she was about three months pregnant with her fourth child, Mary went back to Ireland for a six month visit. Her return trip on the Columbia of the Anchor line would prove to be quite eventful as a baby boy was born to her at sea. The other passengers on the ship adopted her and her family. Women on the ship quickly began to sew clothing for the boy, they looked after her other children while she recuperated, and at the end of the trip the passengers presented her with $200 which was reported to have given Mary quite a smile! This event caused quite a stir and was reported first in the New York American paper in New York City and was repeated in full text in the Greenwich Journal. The paper reported that the boy was christened Dennis Columbia O'Hanlon. Mary's husband had remained in Greenwich to "tend to business." Whether her husband did not like the name or the paper had the name wrong, because the boy is called Stephen O'Hanlon in all other references.
Thomas Wilson	Thomas Wilson made a return trip to Ireland in 1899. A copy of Thomas' passport is included here.

Joseph J. Henderson	Joseph went back to Ireland on a recruiting trip around 1908. On this trip he was able to convince William George Jackson to come to Greenwich.
John G. McMaster and wife	Took several trips to Ireland before finally returning to Ireland in 1888. They went to Ireland 21 Jun 1883 and stayed there for the summer returning 5 Sept 1883. During their absence, Acheson A. McMaster acted as mill manager. Acheson later became an Anglican priest and served a congregation in West Hartlepool, County Durham, England. John and his wife made a second trip 22 Aug 1885 and returned to Greenwich after a few weeks. On 7 Apr 1888 John and his wife returned to Ireland never to return again. The poor health of John was the reason given. It was hoped that returning to Ireland would help his condition. Unfortunately it did not help as he died in Ireland in October 1889.
Hugh Dunbar McMaster	He came to Greenwich in early 1880 to directly oversee the setup of operations. In May he returned to Ireland. He made nearly annual visits through 1898. His first annual visit was in June of 1881. The Journal stated that they would like it if the senior member of the firm of Dunbar, McMaster, and Co. would make Greenwich his permanent home. This idea never came to pass.
Mr and Mrs. Wm Mulligan	Took a trip with their son to Ireland and returned to Greenwich in August 1909.
Sarah Black	She and her family were living in Greenwich in 1925 having been resident for about two years. Apparently she returned to Gilford, Ireland in about 1926. Her death there in 1937 was reported in the Journal.
Mary and Belle Curry	They returned to Ireland around 1919 for about 10 months. Then they came back and lived out their days in Greenwich.
Joseph Adamson	At the outbreak of World War I, Joseph was determined to serve even before the United States entered the conflict. To do so he returned to Ireland and joined the British army. During the war he was taken as a prisoner. He died in a German prison in Hams, France 6 Jun 1918.

Alice McLean	After living in Greenwich for several years she returned to Ireland 10 Jun 1911 on board the California. She made Ireland her permanent home.
Martha Emerson	Took passage to Ireland 10 Jun 1911 on board the California with Alice McLean. Martha came back to Greenwich after a several weeks visit.
Mrs. Robert Mulligan	She left in July 1884 for a two month visit to see her parents in Ireland.
William E. Simms	He sent his wife and daughter to Ireland to visit with his family in the summer of 1914.
James Shields	Left in April of 1911 to spend several months in Ireland.
Wm C. Seaton	He and his daughter left 13 Sept 1884 for a six week visit to Ireland. They returned on 20 Sept 1884.

On Sending Money Home to Ireland

It was apparently the custom to send some of the earnings home to Ireland to help out. This practice was acknowledged in the <u>Journal</u> when the rates for foreign money orders went up in 1911.

Picking Up the Immigrants and The Two Dogs

It was a custom of the Dunbarton to send one of its workers to New York city to greet arriving workers. According to Jane Whitaker, her grandfather, Joseph Chambers did this regularly.

In 1892, Ellis Island, located in New York Harbor, was established as a major processing point for immigrants. The purpose of this check in was to assure that those coming into this country were healthy and were not carrying any infectious diseases.

At one time my Great Grandfather, George Ruddock, was asked to go and pick up some arrivals. The family came with two ceramic dogs as their prize possession. Unfortunately one of the family had consumption (tuberculosis) and was denied entry into the United States. Sad and bewildered they were sent back to Ireland. As a way of thanking George, they gave him the two dogs. These gifts remain in the possession of George's grandson, Gilbert Ruddock.

Chapter XII - Dunbarton's Businessmen

William J. Wilson and the Westwood Park

William J. Wilson, the son of Joseph and Eliza (Sturgeon) Wilson, was born near Gilford, Ireland. He first came to the United States to work in Chicago, Illinois around 1882. Shortly thereafter he moved to Greenwich where he first worked in the Dunbar, McMaster & Co. mill in Greenwich as a foreman in the preparing department.

In February of 1890 he purchased property at the corner of Bleeker and John Streets and built a tenement house there. He later added on to this tenement house with a grocery store. The location of this store was ideal for many of the mill's employees because workers from Bleeker, John, and Washington would pass this store going to and from work. To run this store he entered into a partnership with Peter Bradley in February 1901 under the name of Wilson and Bradley.

Mr. Wilson was the first person associated with the mill to get elected to the village board as a trustee. This position he held for the years 1898 - 1902. He was also a trustee of the United Presbyterian church.

William J. Wilson became a large property owner in Greenwich. He purchased a farm on the Easton side of the Kill across and down stream from the Dunbarton. In the summer of 1909, the Dunbarton needed to re-build its dam which was taken out by spring floods. To re-build this dam, the Dunbarton needed a little property on the Easton side. William J. Wilson was able to negotiate a trade with the Dunbarton for some property on the Greenwich side just downstream from the Dunbarton. In December of 1909, with property on both sides of the river, he undertook the task of building a bridge across the Batten Kill.

Initially he intended to build this bridge just to shorten by one and a half miles the distance from his farm to his village residence on John street. The bridge was a suspension bridge designed for foot travel. It was built with four one-inch steel cables which hung over firm supports of timber on either side. The planks were laid on other cables which were suspended from these. To make the bridge he hired several men to prepare the approaches on either side and to build supporting piers on both sides of the Kill.

In the Journal of 23 May 1911, William announced that anyone wishing to walk through his farm could cross the bridge for a nickel on Memorial Day. He called his farm the Westwood Park and set up some nice trails through the woods. On 31 May, Memorial Day, he collected more than 700 nickels for the privilege to cross his bridge and experience the Park! The festivities began with the Band marching across the bridge. Apparently a total of 16 members marched in time to the snare drum causing the bridge to vibrate quite a bit. The shaking bridge was also a concern to William Wilson who asked that it not be repeated. Once across, the band was followed by many of the citizens of Greenwich. On the other side of the river the band played several dance numbers and the young people of the town enjoyed dancing. Apparently the only complaint about the Park was the lack of food.

Westwood Park had a short life because W. J. Wilson died in July of 1911 and there is no record of the Park being used again.

Joseph Lyttle

Joseph Lyttle was born in Gilford, Ireland the son of William Lyttle and his first wife Sarah Rice. He came to Greenwich around 1886 to work in the Dunbarton. Joseph's brother James Lyttle had arrived as part of the first group of immigrants in 1880. As was the custom James helped Joseph with passage to America. In the 1892 census he is listed a laborer. By the time he died in 1943, Joseph was a considerable property owner and business man. How did this happen? In the words of one person I interviewed: "Every thing that Joe touched turned to gold."

Joseph Lyttle

Sarah (Donnally) Lyttle

I suspect there was quite a bit of luck involved, but I also believe that Joe was very enterprising. Apparently Joe began by going door to door with groceries after work at the Dunbarton. In May of 1895 Joseph purchased the tea shop of C. W. Mulligan. Eventually he built a grocery store and a grist mill on lower Hill street. In later years this mill would be operated by his son Joseph Lyttle, Jr. It appears that Joe made a habit of purchasing property that no one else wanted and made it into something. Some examples:

1) On property just west of his grist mill he helped establish the Manhattan Shirt company.

2) After prohibition, which made hotel property less valuable, he purchased the American House and improved it and sold it to T. R. Becker.

3) He purchased the Central House and converted it to business use.

4) He purchased the two or three usually vacant small wooden buildings on the corner of Main and Washington streets and established a successful garage and service station.

5) He purchased a farm just south of Middle Falls in Easton. To most this looked just like any other farm. On this farm was a ledge of rock which was called "cement mountain". It turned out that this mountain was made of limestone which was particularly valuable in the production of macadam and cement. In 1933 more than forty-five men were employed in the quarrying of the limestone. This deposit was still being mined in the early 1970s.

6) In June 1927, he and his sons leased property at the corner of John Street and VanNess (just kitty-corner to the Dunbarton main gate) to establish a Coal business. Joseph's son William J. Lyttle was the manager of this new venture. This business continues to this day as Lyttle Oil Company.

7) He purchased Palmer's mill in Mill Hollow in May of 1933 including the all its tenement houses as well. This mill was the site of numerous industries before and after his purchase.

One of the first properties Joseph Lyttle was able to sell was property on Hill Street just east of where he later would build his grist mill. This lot sold for $200.00 in November of 1897 to the Greenwich and Easton Elgin Butter and Cheese factory.

Joseph moved from mill laborer to mill owner. In essence he lived and proved the American dream. Through hard work and perseverance one can rise above one's born station in life.

James Wallace and The Linen Underwear Mill

In June of 1903 a separate company was formed by James W. Wallace, Managing Director of the Dunbarton Flax Spinning Company, LeRoy Thompson of Greenwich, John Doan of Cooperstown, New York and H. M. Sweet of Cohoes, New York. This mill was established to produce linen underwear as its name designates. The site of the mill was chosen at the corner of Corliss and Main Streets in Greenwich. It was here that a two story mill was built 80 by 36 feet. The garments produced here had never been extensively produced in the United States as they were mostly imported. Such underwear brought a price as high as $3.25 per article.

While this mill was as separate company from the Dunbarton, many of the Dunbarton's workers and family found employment in this new mill.

This mill operated until 1942, shortly after the death of L. G. Thompson, the son of one of the founders, when it went out of business.

Chapter XIII - Some Memories Around Town

Memories of Ike Jackson

When I asked Ike Jackson for some background information on the Dunbarton he was kind enough to write what follows. It is written in first person and Ike is speaking:

My first memories of the Dunbarton mill were the mill whistle and the tall picket fence that surrounded the property. I estimate that I would have been 3 to 5 years old and my birthday is 9/18/19. The whistle was operated with steam. It projected out of the roof of the boiler house and was clearly visible through the picket fence. At that time the whistle blew three times each day Monday through Saturday. The times were 7:00 am, 12:00 noon, and 5:00 pm. The fireman in the boiler house was responsible. He actuated the blow by pulling a chain which went from the boiler room floor to a lever valve near the roof. Samuel Crozier, Sr. was the fireman's name.

It was a fascinating sight to see the whistle belch a Huge cloud of steam and to listen to the sound which could be heard all over the village.

The picket fence was approximately eight feet tall. It was what one thinks of when "picket fence" is spoken. The pickets were of wood, about 1" x 3" by 8 ft and pointed to shed the rain and discourage climbing. The entire fence was painted gray. There were several gates through [the] fence which were locked with pad locks and chains. The main gate at the "top of [the] hill" [at the end of Corliss Ave] consisted of an arched structure with two wide swinging gates. Adjacent to this was an employee gate. There were a couple of simple benches inside the gates where the men sat and talked before "punching in." A building further down the hill served as the place were the employees punched their cards "in" and "out". This same building served as a lunch room for those who carried their lunches.

Many of the employees went home for lunch. The lunch hour was one hour and most lived within easy walking distance in the west end of Greenwich. Living close to work was a necessity. There were few cars.

There was a railroad siding and a row of mill houses outside the fenced yard. These were located to the west of the main railroad line and the railroad depot. At the end of the spur a trestle was constructed over an excavated level where trucks could back under the coal cars. The boilers were fired with soft coal. The coal was carted load by load down into the mill yard and unloaded onto a large storage pile. The fireman had to keep the fire stoked and move coal from the storage pile into the boiler room. This was done with a shovel and a wheelbarrow. Another duty of the fireman was to remove the ash and clinkers. The ash was removed from [the] ash pit with long handled hoes, made entirely of steel. They were wheeled to the ash pile in a wheel barrow. The mill operated one shift for many years and later went to a second shift. The firemen were responsible for the duties mentioned above and a third man worked the down time shift to keep the fire alive and serve as a watchman. The watchman made regular rounds with a punch clock. It served two purposes, it provided security and kept the watchman awake. He had a few security plans of his own which let him capture a couple of winks. He threw a blanket in the empty wheel barrow, set an alarm clock once each hour and relaxed with his paper. The steam power was for a large stationary Corliss steam engine. It was an alternate source of power with water power. More will be written on this.

I would like to back up to where this started and add some background about my family. My father George Jackson, provided me with the memories written here. He immigrated to the USA and Greenwich to work in the Dunbarton Flax Spinning Co. He left my mother Sarah Swan Stewart Jackson, my brother William [(Stoney)], and Sister Sarah [(Sadie)] in Bessbrook, Northern Ireland until he was able to provided passage for them to come to the USA. William and Sarah reside in Greenwich, New York at this writing. There were two other brothers, John and George, now deceased. Sister Dorothy also resides in Greenwich.

My father had served an apprenticeship in Ireland, in the linen manufacturing industry. This experience provided him with the opportunity to come to the USA and Greenwich. His duties over the years were machinery installation, maintenance and overall plant maintenance of a mechanical nature. He had one job during his lifetime in Greenwich. This was at the Dunbarton.

The Jackson family grew up in a small company-owned farm house just outside the fenced-in mill yard. My father's work required that he be readily available for problems of a mechanical nature. This resulted in many trips to the mill during work hours and during the down time hours. Quite often during these down hours he would invite me to "go to the mill" with him. Obviously the safety rules were much more lenient in those days. It was during these visits to the mill that I learned how the mill manufactured linen shoe thread and broom twine, the two principal products.

Back to the power sources:

The mill was built on the Batten kill river to take advantage of the drop in elevation from its source in Vermont to its end in the Hudson river. The mill dam was built across the river where it curved around the south west corner of the village. The mill pond above the dam extended up river for about a quarter mile and doubled the width. The dam was about eight foot high. During the summer months, when water levels tend to be lower, splash boards were run across the dam top to extend its height. During the down times the dam pond filled back to its required head. During periods of prolonged water shortage the steam engine was used as needed. There were head gates which fed from the pond into two separate raceways. The raceways originally were constructed as underground tunnels that ran across the mill yard. They were constructed of cypress planks and framing. In later years the raceway which ran through the main part of the yard was replaced with one which was constructed of poured concrete. This raceway resembled a canal. It was open, had fencing along the sides and two bridges which gave access to the east end of the mill. Each raceway supplied a turbine type water wheel. The discharge from the water wheel was returned to the river on the south and west end of the plant.

I remember one breakdown which required that a forged patch be fitted to the main gear of the waterwheel. Replacement parts were not readily available. The decision was made to have Lemuel Burgess do this in his blacksmith shop located on lower Corliss Avenue. When one considers that on open forge, an anvil, some tongs and a blacksmith's hammer were the available means of making this patch, it becomes a monumental task. I can picture Lem going down the hill with the heavy steel patch. He would try it for fit, trudge back up the hill to his shop, reheat it to a red-hot malleable condition, forge it with hammer and repeat the trip for another fitting. This went on for days until they finally got the waterwheel back into service.

Waterpower was the power source of choice for obvious reasons. The steam engine required that tons of coal be used to generate steam. It was possible to use steam power and water power at the same time for different sections of the mill. The power was transmitted through large leather belting to a main line shaft and secondary line shafts to the entire mill. Belting from the main line shaft supplied the power for individual machines. Manufacturing machines could be engaged or disengaged as required. Each machine had an operator. To the best of my knowledge all of the operators were women.

The boiler house, the steam engine and the waterwheel room were located adjacent to each other. The machine shop was also located in this part of the plant. The large number of individual machines required a large amount of maintenance and repairs. The drive belts were leather. They stretched, they slipped, they wore out and they broke. Bearings were not the modern ball bearings that we know now. They were friction bearings which required a continuous supply of oil. If a bearing ran out of oil it overheated and created the danger of fire. Machine parts would wear out and require replacements. The machine shop was a busy place. Much of the work was done on off hours.

The shop was equipped with the usual metal turning lathes, drill presses, milling machines, boring mills, power saws, welding equipment (gas) and bench tools. There were some specialized projects related to the business of making thread. I remember one man that turned out wooden pulleys for the machinery where the process started. His name was Robert Mahon. White birch was purchased locally. The logs were about one foot in diameter. They were seasoned for an appropriate time in the mill yard. Slices of a proper thickness were sawed and from there on the pulley took shape on Mr. Mahon's lathe. He was one of those specialists who did the job best.

The manufacturing process started in a room called the "Carding Room". I cannot recall seeing the process of separating the fiber from the natural state. It is possible that this could have taken place in the room that I know as the "Dye house". This room contained tanks, many individual tubs and equipment that would be associated with the rendering of the fiber from the stalk. I recall huge bales wrapped in burlap coming in freight cars. I am sure that must have been the rendered fiber. There wasn't any flax plants grown in this area and I'm sure that it was easier and more economical to buy processed fiber.

The [flax] fiber is long when compared to other natural fibers such as silk and cotton and wool. Women sitting at a "spread board" fed loose fibers down an open topped channel continuously. The channel was approximately six inches wide and six inches deep. The spread board had women on both sides. The women took the fibers from the bales and organized them into a continuous bundle. This was the first step. This bundle was as large as the channel that it traveled in. It was picked up by a carding machine which reduced the overall diameter of the bundle and at the same time oriented the fibers by drawing them through a carding comb. A name that I remember are hackle bars and hackle pins. Hackle pins varied in size and looked exactly like steel sewing needles with one end squared to fit a female receptacle. The hackle bar contained many sockets to hold the hackle pins. When completely assembled it resembled a comb or rake. I believe the carding process required several hackle bars and probably finer sizes. I was always fascinated with ribbons of flax that emerged from the machine and neatly arranged themselves in the tall receptacles. The ribbon of flax was approximately 3/4" wide and 1/16" thick and as soft as a cob web.

I recall seeing many full receptacles in storage waiting for the next operation. The ribbons were reduced in size by separating them into much smaller ribbons and eventually twisting them into strands.

The finished shoe thread consisted of several strands twisted into a larger thread (approx. .030" dia). The broom twine was smaller in diameter because fewer strands made up the thread. The finished thread was incredibly strong. The twisted strand construction combined with the long fiber made a soft flexible thread. I can recall strong men testing their strength against the strength of the thread. A loop was put around each hand with slack between. I don't recall anyone breaking the thread. The thread strength coupled with the tightening into the flesh of the hands made it a nearly impossible task.

I can't remember the exact routine of operations after "twisting". At this point the thread physically had reached its final condition or shape. However other operations were performed and I will offer my understanding.

The twisted thread was collected into large hanks or coils and stored by hanging them on arms that projected horizontally. The hanging coil was about three to four feet long. There was one building apart from the manufacturing that stood on piers about six foot above the ground. Underneath this building were horizontal poles for hanging the hanks of thread for drying and storage.

Aging could have been another use. I expect that this open air drying operation was for a relatively short period.

The "dye house" was located on the south west corner of the property close to the river. As the name would indicate the thread or broom twine was dyed here. I don't recall the shoe thread being any color other than off white unbleached linen, while the broom twine was dyed to brighter colors.

There were many rectangular shaped tubs or "vats" lining the walls. The tubes were set side by side in pairs so that the mechanical device mounted above them could be powered by the same belt driven power source from the main shaft. This mechanical structure above the tubs had horizontal (wooden) arms which rotated above the center of their own axis. Hanks of thread were draped on these arms with the bottom of the hank being immersed in the liquid in the tub. When the arms turned the hanks traveled into and out of the liquid in an endless manner. The tubs had steam pipes in the liquid to raise the temperature. I have no knowledge as to what the liquids in the tubs were.

There were other large metal tanks with hinged lids and also heated by steam. The dye house always seemed like a wet steamy place. The floors were wet, the windows steamed and it had a strange odor.

After the dying process was completed the hanks were moved to another place called the "drying loft." This room had provisions for holding the hanks on poles similar to the description above. This room was located above and close to the boiler room. It was also equipped with steam heat. The room picked up passive heat from the boiler room nearby and augmented this with steam coils.

At some point in the total operation the hanks of thread had to be transferred onto bobbins. This was done to get it into a form which was more manageable in the last step of manufacturing called "spinning". As you might guess this was done in the "Spinning room". I never understood why the final operation was called spinning. The thread was level wound onto a heavy paper board core. The core did not have flanges on each end as a spool for thread does. This meant that the thread boundaries had to be perfectly square with the axis. There were many cores on the spinning machine and they rotated at high speed. A level winding device traveled quickly back and fourth laying down a beautiful pattern on the core.

The finished spool was about three inches in diameter and five inches long. They were tightly wound and stacked nicely on end. As in other processes the machine operators were women.

A spool of thread from the Dunbarton mill. In the 1940s and 1950s employees of the mill wore buttons like this one. Button and spool in possession of Raymond Lang.

The finished product was shipped by freight on box cars. The box cars were loaded on the mill siding and initially transported by the Greenwich and Johnsonville Railroad.

Along towards the end of world war I the Dunbarton mill built a day care center for the employee families. It was called the "Nursery". It is presently the home of Dorothy Jackson on lower Corliss Ave. The house and provided care were directed towards the children while the mothers and fathers were at work. The first and second floors were identical. Each floor had a parlor, a large activity room , a kitchen and bath. Each floor had a large porch on the front. The basement had five bathrooms (with tubs) and a separate shower. The heating plant was located in the basement. The basement was nicely finished and I would guess that the laundry was down in this area. The basement floor was at ground level and opened into a backyard. In later years the "Nursery" was converted into a two family residence.

My boyhood years were closely related to the happening in the mill, the west end of Greenwich and the Batten Kill river. I have fond memories of fishing below the dam, in the raceway discharges and across the river at the "eddy". My father taught me how to fish, to dig worms, to catch bait fish, to catch grasshoppers, and how to clean the fish for dinner. We always had a handmade boat to get across the river and into the woods. We knew when it was time to go home, the mill whistle told us.

Finally, we think of the early years and compare them with our modern life style and "cherish" our memories.

Ike Jackson

Memories of Two of Ireland's Own

At the time of publication, to the knowledge of the author, there were only two living Dunbarton workers who were born in Ireland. They were Ivy Cooke Brown Cahill who came over as a girl with her mother and Jane Feenan Connors who came over as an adult. Sarah (Skiff) Idleman, a life long resident of the Greenwich area and an 8th grade history teacher, has a keen interest in gathering up the oral histories of the people of the Dunbarton. What follows here are the memories of Ivy and Jane as recorded by Sarah.

Ivy Cooke Brown Cahill

Ivy B. Cahill was born in 1911 in Belfast, Northern Ireland. She emigrated to the United States in 1920 with her mother, Rachel Courtney, siblings, Thomas and William Cooke, and Sarah Courtney. They joined another brother, Jimmy Cooke, and three sisters, Frances, Elizabeth and Rachel Cooke, who lived in Greenwich. Jimmy, William and Rachel all worked in the Dunbarton. Ivy attended school in Greenwich until she was 16. She left school in 1927 to work in the Dunbarton. She stayed on until 1945.

[School] was difficult. I made it difficult, probably because I'm stubborn and I say the thing and I'll stick by it. I told you I wasn't a good student, a perfect student, an honor student. Many's the welt I had on these hands. They used to take the tires and cut them up. A rubber strap. A lot of times I didn't deserve it, but I never said. I fought my way through there. I got as far as eighth grade. I wanted to quit school, I wanted to be on my own.

I went to the Dunbarton when I was sixteen for 50 cents an hour. I went in at 6 and went until 1:30. They laughed when I went in a doffer. My brothers were all big shots there and I was a doffer.

I went to work doffin', yep, that's a starter. The doffer takes the spindles off the machine when it's full and runs like hell and gets more empty bobbins and brings the bobbins in and puts 'em on the spindles. I think there's four machines to one tender and I think there was 80 bobbins. There was four doffers for all the machines, taking the bobbins off and putting on the new ones. The girls [doffers] sat at the end and when one machine was ready the girl that was running [the machine] wanted you to get the hell in there and get those bobbins off, get fresh ones on so she could start it up again.

When they [the machines] were all going you didn't talk very much. You had a few minutes, a very few minutes, every now and then. One machine would stop if you're doffin' it, maybe another one would stop and she'd be hammering and hammering, "Come to me, come to me, get my machine going." Doffin' was hard, especially if you're small, you know. And the bobbins are heavy. How long was I there as a doffer? Quite a while, quite a while. I was too long on it and I hated it.

I went from doffin' to spinnin'. I worked a long time as a spinner, as long as I worked in the Dunbarton. Spinnin' is on the same frames, only a better job. Maybe I worked a little while helping out as a back tender. That was another good job. Two good jobs and everybody laughed about it. They laughed when I went in a doffer. My brothers were all big shots there and I was a doffer.

I made good on the spinnin'. It was hard because I was short, disadvantage of reaching the yarn, you know, to pull it through. The back tenders bring in the flax already to spin, raw flax. It's on carts and they put it in cylinders and it comes out of that cylinder up over bobbin after boddin after bobbin, steel bobbins, you know. The machine is running and it brings it down through and it's combing it and softening it. And it comes down through as thread.

It's terrible dirty, very oily, greasy and the machinery is heavy. It's hard work. You got cuts, twine cuts, deep and sore. I got one [a scar] to show. I was cutting the lap off the spinner machine. The knife slipped off the thing, you know. Scared the life out of me. I was out of work for two weeks and never got paid. Never got anything unless it was on your face. The Dunbarton's a tough job, all the way through.

My brothers did very well in the Dunbarton, they come up the steps there very well. All had good positions, one was a manager and the other one was a foreman. I went in to work there and got the poorest job in the mill. The girls, of course, were workers. But the men, did very well and were promoted.

The mill wasn't unionized. Joe Richie and George Daisy was against it. They tried to unionize it from Paterson but it never was. There was a strike [in Greenwich]. Johnny Nolan and that bunch worked in the reeling room. Something was unfair in the reeling room and they wanted more money. Johnny Nolan's outfit went on strike. But some of them didn't, they reneged on it. It lasted quite a while. I could go out on strike if I'd wanted to, but I didn't see any cause to go. I was on my own. There was no money if you didn't work. And my brothers, high up on a row, said, "You're not striking!"

There was a fight in front of the mill. I got hell knocked out of me there too, but I gave back as much as I got. Alice McLean come up behind me and knocked me. She was a big, heavy woman. Jesus, she hurt me. I didn't see her, [she] hit me over the head with an umbrella. So I took the umbrella and broke it over her head. She was mad because she was on strike and I wasn't. Jimmy Ryan tried to stop me from fighting, son of a bitch, but I fought. There was a fight in front of the mill and in front of the house getting off the bus. If they could get you anywhere, they would.

But they [the Dunbarton] got the deputy and the bus to take us in to work, which was nice. My brother Jimmy, the Flynn girls and Rosie Nolan went on the bus. You were safe then. Nothin' came of it and the workers was glad when it was over.

Jane Feenan Connor

Jane Connor was born in 1914 in Newry, County Armagh, Northern Ireland. At the age of 14, she went to work as a yarn reeler in the Black Staff Spinning Mill. In 1946, she emigrated to this country and settled in Greenwich with her older brother, Chris Feenan, and his wife, Bridget. A week after her arrival, she began work at the Linen Thread Company, formerly known as the Dunbarton Flax Spinning Company. She worked there until it closed in 1952.

Chris [Feenan] brought me over in 1946 - lived with him and his wife, Bridget. He took me up to see George Daisy and we had a conference. I came here on a Thursday and it was on a Friday and they wanted me to go to work on a Monday. But Chris said, "No, we're going to give her some time to be home." So I went to work a week after that.

I went to work in the Dunbarton Mill. It belonged to another mill in County Armagh - Northern Ireland. We had only two shifts, 6 in the morning to 1:30 and 1:30 to 10. One week you'd work 6 to 1:30. The other week you'd work 1:30 to 10. I only took home $28 dollars a week. I paid $10 for my board and $10 for my passage to Chris. We had a thing called bees. You went over a quota it was called a bee. They'd put it up on the wall and you got maybe a dollar and half or something like that. You'd get extra pay for so many bees. But it was nothing, silly old thing. It wasn't worth it, I never took home any more than $28.

The first room would be the preparing room. That's where they made all the tow. Old Billy Burns was the boss of the preparing room. He was Protestant and didn't like Catholics. I was doing a special for Patterson, New Jersey and I was working on yellow lisem, real yellow. I always had to ask him and said to him one day, "I gotta have some lisem, I don't have no more." He came down and had it drooped across his shoulders. I said, "Don't you think you're getting too old for the twelfth of July?" [Protestant holiday in Ireland]. He thought I didn't remember, see. Oh, we had a lot of fun. Oh yes, yes!

After the preparing room, then it went over to the spreadboard. Raw tow it used to come in burlap bags, big burlap bags. Rachel Murphy, Mrs. Kopa, Kitty McConnell and all them used to work on the spreadboard. It was a square board and it was all needles. It was a dangerous job. Over in Ireland we had girl went through the spreader, you know. The tow came in lumps. They us to have to take it out in hand fulls and spread it and work till it would come out and be as white as that. Then they put it in cans and then it would go upstair; the winders and the twisters and was made into cord.

The spinning part of the mill and the reeling part were all in one big room. I worked in the reeling loft and that's where we made the yarn, wind-around-yarn, you know.

There were four frames and there's ten bobbins to a frame and you took care of them. Over in Ireland I worked a reel that had 32 ends and a footboard all the way across. All you had to do to stop it was take your foot off the footboard and it stopped right away. They had levers on the reel. You could always shut it off with the lever. But when I come here first we didn't have no levers on them reels. I came home one night and I had such black and blue knees from putting my knee up to stop it, you know. I showed my knees to Mr. Richie one morning. I said, "I couldn't work like that!" So finally, they got levers on the reels. When they got the levers, it was good. The owners were good at doing anything you wanted them to do.

In back of me was the spinning frames where they used to spin the yarn that came from the big cans downstairs. Patty Murphy was manager, boss of the spinnin'. Owen Murphy, working in the dye house, used to come up and take it to the loft to have it all dyed.

Then it would go back downstairs again to where Mary McConnell worked and it was all packaged in cord like to send to the stores. My sister Mary [Stiles] used to package that, it was lovely and white. Oh God, they were crazy about her down there, she was a character.

That's where I took out my first Blue Cross and Blue Shield. It only cost me a dollar and something a month. Ken Kelly was the one that took care of it. He told me you can't work here if you don't have Blue Cross and Blue Shield. I said, "What in the hell is that?" He said, "It"s medical." I said, "OK."

Sometimes the Dunbarton in Ireland wanted a special. Somethin' that they (Dunbar, McMaster and Co. in Belfast, Ireland] were trying new would be a special. I always done it up in Greenwich. They gave me two reels over by myself where we used to do the specials. I used to be scared to death. I was afraid of doin' something wrong. But they always brought the special up to me. Maybe it was because I come from Ireland.

Sources

Chapter I Flax and the Production of Linen
A Little on Linen and Growing Flax and Processing the Fiber
Sources: The Story of Linen by William F. Leggett published 1945 by Chemical Publishing Co, Inc. Brooklyn, N.Y.; An Introduction to the Study of Spinning by W. E. Morton and G. R. Gray, copyright 1962; Natural and Manmade Textile Fibers Raw Material to Finished Fabric by George E. Linton, published 1966 by Duell, Sloan and Pearce, N.Y.; How to Weave Linens by Edward F. Worst, published 1926 by the Bruce Publishing Company, Milwaukee, WI.; Flax Culture in the United States by E. A. Whitman with introduction by J. R. Leeson published 1888 by Rand Avery Company, Boston, Massachusetts.; Flax in Flanders Throughout the Centuries by Tielt Lannoo, Published 1987 in Belgium translated by Katrien Douchy.

Making Linen Thread From Scutched Flax
Sources: The Story of Linen by William F. Leggett published 1945 by Chemical Publishing Co, Inc. Brooklyn, N.Y.; An Introduction to the Study of Spinning by W. E. Morton and G. R. Gray, copyright 1962; Natural and Manmade Textile Fibers Raw Material to Finished Fabric by George E. Linton, published 1966 by Duell, Sloan and Pearce, N.Y.; How to Weave Linens by Edward F. Worst, published 1926 by the Bruce Publishing Company, Milwaukee, WI.; Picking Up the Linen Threads a Study in Industrial Folklore, by Betty Messenger, University of Texas Press, Austin, 1980.

What Was Made at the Dunbarton
Sources: The Greenwich Journal 13 May 1880; 1 Jul 1880; 15 Apr 1908; Isaac Jackson

Flax Dressers or Hacklers
Sources: United States Trade Commission Tariff Information Surveys for 1891-1924; Flax Culture in the United States, by E. A. Whitman, published by Rand Avery Company, Boston, 1888; Picking Up the Linen Threads, by Betty Messenger, published 1975 University of Texas Press, Austin; "Development of the Dunbarton Mill During its First Decade in Greenwich", by George D. Daisy as found in the Greenwich Journal and Fort Edward Advertizer, 3 Mar 1952; The Greenwich Journal 1 Feb 1899; 1880, 1900, 1910, 1920 US Censuses of Greenwich and Easton, 1892, 1905, 1915, 1925 New York Censuses of Greenwich and Easton; Donald Perkins.

Preparing / Spreading
Sources: Picking Up the Linen Threads by Betty Messenger; 1880, 1900, 1910, 1920 US Censuses of Greenwich and Easton, 1892, 1905, 1915, 1925 New York Censuses of Greenwich and Easton; Donald Perkins.

Spinners, Reelers, Rovers and Doffers

Sources: <u>Picking Up the Linen Threads</u> by Betty Messenger; 1880, 1900, 1910, 1920 US Censuses of Greenwich and Easton, 1892, 1905, 1915, 1925 New York Censuses of Greenwich and Easton; Donald Perkins.

Twisting

Sources: <u>Picking Up the Linen Threads</u> by Betty Messenger; 1880, 1900, 1910, 1920 US Censuses of Greenwich and Easton, 1892, 1905, 1915, 1925 New York Censuses of Greenwich and Easton; Donald Perkins.

Winders

Sources: <u>Picking Up the Linen Threads</u> by Betty Messenger; 1880, 1900, 1910, 1920 US Censuses of Greenwich and Easton, 1892, 1905, 1915, 1925 New York Censuses of Greenwich and Easton; Donald Perkins.

The Dye House workers

Sources: <u>Picking Up the Linen Threads</u> by Betty Messenger; 1880, 1900, 1910, 1920 US Censuses of Greenwich and Easton, 1892, 1905, 1915, 1925 New York Censuses of Greenwich and Easton; Donald Perkins.

Finishing Room

Sources: <u>Picking Up the Linen Threads</u> by Betty Messenger; 1880, 1900, 1910, 1920 US Censuses of Greenwich and Easton, 1892, 1905, 1915, 1925 New York Censuses of Greenwich and Easton; Donald Perkins.

The Boiler House

Sources: <u>Picking Up the Linen Threads</u> by Betty Messenger; 1880, 1900, 1910, 1920 US Censuses of Greenwich and Easton, 1892, 1905, 1915, 1925 New York Censuses of Greenwich and Easton; Donald Perkins.

The Two Master Mechanics and The Mechanics and Wood Turners

Sources: Isaac Jackson, Dorothy Jackson, Sarah (Jackson) Skiff; Joseph Wever; <u>Through the Years a History of the United Presbyterian Church of Greenwich</u> 1955; Naturalization records of Washington County; Donald Perkins; 1880, 1900, 1910, 1920 US Censuses of Greenwich and Easton, 1892, 1905, 1915, 1925 New York Censuses of Greenwich and Easton.

The Office Workers

Sources: <u>Picking Up the Linen Threads</u> by Betty Messenger; 1880, 1900, 1910, 1920 US Censuses of Greenwich and Easton, 1892, 1905, 1915, 1925 New York Censuses of Greenwich and Easton; Donald Perkins; Shirley (Garrett) Friday.

The Management of the Mill

Sources: 1880, 1900, 1910, 1920 US Censuses; 1892, 1905, 1915, 1925 New York Censuses; <u>The Greenwich Journal</u> 17 May 1883; 6 Sept 1883; 15 Jan 1885; 29 Mar 1888; 9 Jan 1901; 12 Aug 1903; 6 Oct 1909; 20 Oct 1909; 18 Aug 1915; 20 Mar 1918; 10 Sept 1919; 7 Jul 1920; 2 Nov 1921; 26 May 1926

The Agents

Sources: <u>Zell's United States Business Directory</u> of 1881; <u>The People's Journal</u> June 2, 1892; <u>The Greenwich Journal</u> 15 Sept 1897; 1 Dec 1897

Sources of Flax

Sources: <u>Greenwich Journal</u> dated 1 Apr 1880; 26 Aug 1880; 12 Aug 1880; 10 Jun 1880; 16 Dec 1914; 9 Oct 1940; 16 Oct 1940

Cotton vs Linen

Sources: <u>Natural and Manmade Textile Fibers Raw Material to Finished Fabric</u> by George E. Linton, published 1966 by Duell, Sloan, and Pearce, New York

Flax and Washington and Rensselaer Counties

Sources: <u>Flax Culture in the United States</u> by E. A. Whitman with introduction by J. R. Leeson published 1888 by Rand Avery Company, Boston, Massachusetts.; <u>A Historical, Topological, and Agricultural Survey of the County of Washington</u>, by Asa Fitch, Published about 1849; <u>The Greenwich Journal</u> 10 Jun 1880; 16 Dec 1914; 9 Oct 1940; 16 Oct 1940

The Flax and Hemp Growers and Spinners Association

Sources: <u>The Greenwich Journal</u> 20 Jul 1882; 22 Feb 1883; 25 Feb 1887

Chapter II - The history of the Dunbarton

General Time Line of Events

Sources: <u>The People's Journal</u> 4 Sept 1879; 30 Oct 1879; 15 Jan 1880; 19 Feb 1880; 26 Feb 1880; 18 Mar 1880;1 Apr 1880; 8 Apr 1880; 15 Apr 1880; 29 Apr 1880; 20 May 1880; 10 Jun 1880; 24 Jun 1880; 1 Jul 1880; 5 Aug 1880; 12 Aug 1880; 9 Sept 1880

History of the Dunbarton Mill in Brief

Sources: 1880 US census of Greenwich and the <u>Journal</u>

1879 - 1880 The First Year

Sources: <u>The Peoples Journal</u> see dates in text

The First Batch of Workers

Sources: 1880 US census

Greenwich in 1879 - Just before the Mill was purchased

Sources: <u>The People's Journal</u> 9 Oct 1879

Dunbarton Fire Department

Sources: <u>The Greenwich Journal</u> 17 Jun 1880; 12 Feb 1885

Floods

Sources: The <u>Greenwich Journal</u> 8 Apr 1880; 13 May 1880; 14 Apr 1887; 16 Oct 1901; 5 Mar 1902; 7 May 1902; 8 Oct 1902; 9 Sept 1903; 29 Mar 1905; 24 Feb 1909; 20 Mar 1912; 2 Apr 1913; 9 Nov 1927; 5 Jan 1949; Opinion of the Supreme Court, Appellate Division, Third Department, September 9, 1903 "Dunbarton Flax Spinning Co. v. Greenwich & Johnsonville RAILWAY. Co."

Law Suit

Sources: The <u>Greenwich Journal</u> 16 Oct 1901; 5 Mar 1902; 7 May 1902; 8 Oct 1902; 9 Sept 1903; Opinion of the Supreme Court, Appellate Division, Third Department, September 9, 1903 "Dunbarton Flax Spinning Co. v. Greenwich & Johnsonville RAILWAY. Co."

Fire

Sources: <u>The Greenwich Journal</u> 26 Oct 1898; Knowledge of the compiler; Sanborn Maps of the Dunbarton; "Gilford and its Mills by M. P. Campbell in <u>Banbridge & District Historical Society Journal</u> volume two.

The Wind Storm of 1916

Source: The Greenwich Journal 5 Jul 1916
The Strike
Sources: The Greenwich Journal 6 Oct 1937; 27 Oct 1937; 25 May 1938; 8 Feb 1939; 3 Mar 1939; 22 Mar 1939; 27 Sept 1939; 2 Aug 1939; Isaac Jackson, Roma Colby; the reciprocal trade agreement between The United States of America and the United Kingdom dated 17 Nov 1938.
Cutting Back - The Demand Declines
Sources: The Greenwich Journal 25 Jan 1950, 5 Mar 1952; Margaret (Wever) Wilson
1952 - The Year the Mill Closed
Sources: The Greenwich Journal 5 Mar 1952; 12 Mar, 1952; 19 Mar 1952; 6 Aug 1952;13 Aug 1952

Chapter III - Community relationships
Attitude Toward the Irish in the Early Years
Sources: The Greenwich Journal 18 Mar 1880; 6 May 1880; 17 Apr 1884; 19 Mar 1885; 6 Aug 1885; 11 Mar 1886
The Greenwich Cricket Club
Sources: The Greenwich Journal 30 Aug 1883; 13 Sept 1883; 27 Sept 1883; 11 Oct 1883; 22 May 1884; 15 Jun 1884; 26 Jun 1884; 10 Jul 1884; 24 Sept 1885; 3 Jun 1886; 8 Jul 1886; 30 Sept 1886; 21 Oct 1886
Marches and Flute Bands
Sources The Peoples Journal 20 Sept 1888; 18 Oct 1888; 1 Nov 1888; 24 Jan 1889
Social Events Sponsored by the Mill in its First Ten Years
Sources: The Greenwich Journal 24 Nov 1881; 17 Apr 1884; 29 Dec 1887
The Centennial of Greenwich
Source: The Greenwich Journal 18 Aug 1909
Italian and Irish Disagreements
Sources: The Greenwich Journal 3 May 1916; 10 May 1916
Prosperity of the Mill and Greenwich
Sources: The Greenwich Journal 26 May 1881; 27 Oct 1881; 19 Jan 1882; 25 May 1882; 26 Jun 1884; 23 Jul 1885; 4 Feb 1886; 6 Aug 1896; 7 Oct 1896; 5 Oct 1899; 15 Apr 1908; 28 May 1913; 24 Jun 1931; 9 May 1945; 25 Jan 1951
Alcohol
Sources: The Greenwich Journal 12 Feb 1880; 19 Feb 1880; 7 Oct 1880; 23 Jul 1885
Five O'Clock Whistle - Its Parallel
Sources: Five O'Clock Whistle by Ramona Herdman published 1938 by Harper & Brothers Publishers; Helen M. Ruddock; The Greenwich Journal 17 Nov 1897; Isaac Jackson

Chapter IV - Tragedy
The Death of Agnes Devine - the First Tragedy
Sources: The Greenwich Journal 15 Sept 1881; 22 Sept 1881; 17 Nov 1881

Attempted Suicide
Sources: The Greenwich Journal 15 Apr 1886; 7 May 1913; 14 May 1913
The Loss of the Little Child
Sources: Joseph Wever, Isaac Jackson, Hazel Nolan Karp, The Greenwich Journal 2 Aug 1933; 5 Jul 1899
Five Over the Dam
Sources: People's Journal, Thursday, July 14, 1892, July 21, 1892; Mary Lesson Brown

Chapter V - The Mill Itself
A layout of the grounds and Improvements along the way
Sources: Sanborn Maps dated 1884, 1891, 1897, 1907, 1913, 1925, 1941 and 1950; The Greenwich Journal 15 Apr 1880; 13 May 1880; 10 Jun 1880; 14 Apr 1881; 1 Nov 1883; 5 Jul 1888; 31 Jan 1889; 23 Oct 1890; 16 Jul 1891; 28 Mar 1895; 26 Sept 1895; 1 Apr 1896; 6 May 1896; 17 Nov 1897; 5 Oct 1898; 25 Jan 1899; 6 Sept 1899; 13 Sept 1899; 1 May 1901; 29 May 1901; 4 Jun 1902; 28 Jan 1903; 16 Oct 1904; 15 Apr 1908; 18 Jul 1923; 23 Jun 1931; 13 Jul 1932; 17 Aug 1932; Ray Lang; Isaac Jackson
The Mill Dam
Sources: The Greenwich Journal 16 Jun 1909; 21 Jul 1909
The Mill Had a Bell Before it Had a Whistle
Sources: The Greenwich Journal 19 Jul 1924, 20 May 1924; Quarterly Vestry minutes of St. Paul's church of Tuesday 28 Apr 1942; "A History of St. Paul's Episcopal Church of Greenwich, New York" by Rev. James L. Lowery, Jr.
On Communicating With Gilford
Sources: The People's Journal 15 Jan 1880; 17 Nov 1881
The Story of the Mill Property
Sources: Land Records of Washington County, New York; Zells United States 1881 Business Directory; The People's Journal; New York Compiled Laws for 1881 Chapter 160; The People' Journal 12 May 1881
Meets and Bounds Description of the Property
Sources: Washington County, New York Deeds
Production Capacity
Sources: The People's Journal 13 May 1880; 10 Jun 1880; 15 Sept 1897

Chapter VI - Working Conditions of the Mill
General Working Conditions and Work Hours
Sources: Greenwich Journal 25 Sept 1912; 6 Aug 1919; 24 Jun 1931; 3 Mar 1952
Pay
Sources: The Greenwich Journal 23 May 1934;15 Apr 1908; 27 Oct 1937; 3 Mar 1952; 24 Jun 1942
Number of Workers
Sources: The Greenwich Journal 15 Sept 1897; 25 Jan 1899; 26 Jul 1939; 9 May 1945

Child Labor
Sources: The Greenwich Journal 24 Oct 1906; The "Alumni Record" published in the 1931 year book of the Greenwich school.
Accidents and Safety
Sources: The Greenwich Journal 7 Apr 1881; 29 Mar 1883; 24 Dec 1885; 31 Aug 1883; 30 Nov 1898; 18 Apr 1900; 18 Jul 1900; Feb 1922; 10 Dec 1930; 21 Jan 1931; Jane Whitaker.
Longevity - the Old Guard
Sources: The Greenwich Journal 18 Jun 1919, 9 Mar 1927, 20 Jun 1928, 14 Jun 1929, 6 Aug 1930, 2 Jul 1930, 14 Aug 1929; The New York State census of 1925
Longevity - the Twenty-Five Year Club
Sources: The Greenwich Journal 9 May 1945; Twenty-Five Year Club picture in possession of Margaret (Wever) Wilson

Chapter VII - The Companies & Families
The Descent of Companies
Sources: "Gilford and Its Mills" by M. P. Campbell in Banbridge and District Historical Society Journal vol 2.; New Jersey Corporations Records; Delaware Corporations Records; The People's Journal; The Greenwich Journal 13 May 1880; 24 Apr 1901; 11 Sept 1901.
Northern Ireland and Linen
Sources: Domestic Industry in Ireland, By W. H. Crawford, published 1972 by Gill and Macmillan, Dublin; The Linen Trade, Alex J. Warden, published 1864 by Longman, Green, Longman, Roberts & Green, London; The Rise of the Irish Linen Industry, by Conrad Gill, Published 1925 at Oxford by the Clarendon Press; They Wrought Among the Tow: Flax and Linen in County Tyrone, 1750-1900, by Pat McDonnell, Published 1990 by the Ulster Historical Foundation, Belfast
The Dunbar Family
Sources: Banbridge Chronicle 29 Aug 1991; Banbridge and District Historical Society Journal vol 2 page 13-19 "Gilford and Its Mills" by M. P. Campbell; Deed dated 3 Nov 1865 between Jane Dunbar and others to John W. McMaster
The McMaster Family
Sources: Banbridge Chronicle 29 Aug 1991; Banbridge and District Historical Society Journal vol 2 page 13-19 "Gilford and Its Mills" by M. P. Campbell; Zell's 1875 United States Business Directory; Deed Jane Dunbar and others to John W. McMaster 3 Nov 1865; Index of Wills and Administrations of Ireland 1872; 1887; 1889; 1907
Awards of the Dunbar, McMaster & Co
Sources: The Greenwich Journal 25 Feb 1885
The Barbours of Hilden, Ireland and Paterson, New Jersey
Sources: The National Cyclopedia of American Biography Vol 15 dated 1916; Who's Who Vol. 6 1910-11, and 17 1932-1933,; History of Paterson, New Jersey by William Nelson, Published 1920, New York; Paterson, New

Jersey: Its advantages for Manufacturing and Residence, Its Industries, Prominent Men, Banks, Schools, Etc. by Shriner, Charles A. pub 1890 by The Press Print and Pub Co.; "A Portrait of John Dougherty Barbour 1824-1901" by T. Neill published in Lisburn Historical Society Journal v. 5 1984; "The Genesis of the Linen Thread Trade" by H. C. Lawlor published in Ulster Journal of Archeology - 3rd Series vol 6, 1943; The Greenwich Journal 24 Nov 1909

The Linen Thread Company
Sources: "A Portrait of John Dougherty Barbour 1824-1901" by T. Neill published in Lisburn Historical Society Journal v. 5 1984; "The Genesis of the Linen Thread Trade" by H. C. Lawlor published in Ulster Journal of Archeology - 3rd Series vol 6, 1943; "Industry and Manufacturing in Grafton" by Charles E. Knowlton as found in The Grafton History Club Papers; Leading Business Men of Worcester, Massachusetts, held in the Worcester Public Library; History of Grafton, written and published by Frederick Clifton Pierce, 1879; Marvyn Scudder Manual of Extinct and Obsolete Companies Vol 1-4 published 1934.; New York State Business Directory and Gazetteer 1882, by Sampson & Davenport & Co, New York, 1882; New Jersey Department of State, Commercial Recording; 1897 and 1898 Directory of Chicago.

Whatever Happened to the Linen Thread Company?
Sources: The Greenwich Journal Mar 1952; Harry E. Flanders, Sales Manager for Blue Mountain Industries; Wall Street Journal 26 Jan 1959, 29 Jul 1975, 30 Sept 1975; Who Owns Whom in America Vol. 1, 1974 by Simon and Sylvester; 1970 Directory of Corporate Affiliations ; "Certificate of Ownership and Merger merging the Linen Thread Co., Inc. into Indian Head Mills, Inc." on file at the Secretary of State, State of Delaware.

Other United States Linen Manufacturing Concerns
Sources: "A Spool of Thread and How it is Made" by Charles H. Clark published for Scribners Monthly, 1879. Flax Culture in the United States by E. A. Whitman with introduction by J. R. Leeson published 1888 by Rand Avery Company, Boston, Massachusetts; Fall River and Its Industries: an Historical and Statistical Record of Village, Town and City., by Henry Hilliard Earl, published New York, Atlantic Publishing and Engraving Co.,; Fall river, B. Earl and Son 1877; The People's Journal 19 Jan 1882

Chapter VIII - On Religion and Faith

Catholic - Protestant
Sources: The Greenwich Journal 26 Jun 1890; 23 Jun 1892; 1880, 1900, 1910, 1920 United States Censuses; Catholic Cemetery Records; Greenwich Cemetery Records

St. Joseph's Parish
Sources: The Greenwich Journal 27 Jul 1882; 13 Jun 1906; Saint Joseph Parish Greenwich, New York by Joseph L. Shannon, O.S.A.

The United Presbyterian Church
Sources: The Greenwich Journal 1 Apr 1880; 29 Apr 1880; 7 Apr 1881; 15

Mar 1883; 8 may 1884; 10 Mar 1897; William T. Ruddock; Through the Years the History of the First Seventy-Five Years of the United Presbyterian Church of Greenwich, New York 1880 - 1955.

St Paul's Episcopal Church
Sources: "A History of St. Paul's Episcopal Church of Greenwich, New York - being an unvarnished, biased, and uninhibited account of happenings within the parish boundaries" by the Rev. James. L. Lowery, Jr. 1966; The People's Journal 8 Apr 1880; 6 May 1880; 21 Apr 1881; 14 Dec 1882; 13 Apr 1882; St. Paul's vestry minutes of 28 Apr 1942.

Chapter IX - On Housing and Child Care
On Owning Your Own Home
Source: People's Journal 6 Apr 1882; 1900, 1910, and 1920 US census.
Greenwich Before and After the Dunbarton
Sources: 1920 US Census; 1866 map of Greenwich
McMaster's Tenement
Sources: Ray Lang, Hazel Nolan Karp, The Greenwich Journal 13 May 1880; 8 Oct 1919; 17 Dec 1919; Shirley (Garrett) Friday
The Castle
Sources: Journal 25 Jun 1883; 14 May 1947; Pat (Burkin) Jackson
19 Corliss Ave
Sources: Carol Hand; Jack Crozier
The Superintendent's house
Sources: 1900, 1910, 1920 US census; Florence (Simms) Amos
The House on Washington Square
Sources: Valentine Wilson Binger
The Day Care Center
Sources: Isaac Jackson, The Greenwich Journal 17 Dec 1919

Chapter X - War and the Dunbarton
The Spanish American War
Sources: The Greenwich Journal 4 May 1898; 15 Jun 1898; 21 Jun 1898; 30 May 1900
World War I
Sources: The Greenwich Journal dated 4 Oct 1916; 27 Jun 1917; 9 Jan 1918; 23 Jan 1918; 30 Jan 1918; 22 May 1918; 18 Dec 1918; 13 Nov 1918; 12 Feb 1919; 23 Apr 1919; 16 Jul 1919; 19 Nov 1919; 25 Feb 1920; 27 Jul 1921; 18 Nov 1925; 18 Aug 1928; Gilbert Ruddock
World War II
Sources: The Greenwich Journal 24 Jun 1942; 11 Apr 1945

Chapter XI - Immigration - Relationships in Ireland
Immigration
Sources: Ike Jackson; Jane Feenan Connors; census records; naturalization records. Advertisement of Andrew McBrinn
Naturalization

Sources: Naturalization records of Washington County, New York.

Some Who Came and Returned

Sources: Jack Crozier, Margaret Crozier Smith, Evelyn Doubleday, Wilson V. Binger, The Greenwich Journal 26 May 1881; 17 May 1883; 21 Jun 1883; 6 Sept 1883; 15 May 1884; 17 Jul 1884; 4 Sept 1884; 23 Sept 1884; 23 Apr 1885; 27 Aug 1885; 7 Jul 1887; 4 Aug 1887; 29 Mar 1888; 14 Jun 1899; 22 May 1902; 26 Apr 1911; 31 May 1911; 18 Dec 1918; 10 Mar 1920; 8 Sept 1937.

On Sending Money Home to Ireland

Sources: Greenwich Journal 18 Jan 1911

Picking Up the Immigrants and The Two Dogs

Sources: Helen M. Ruddock, Jane Whitaker

Chapter XII - Dunbarton's Businessmen

William J. Wilson and the Westwood Park

Sources: Wilson Binger; The Greenwich Journal 13 Feb 1890; 20 Feb 1901; 29 Dec 1909; 24 May 1911; 31 May 1911; 19 Jul 1911

Joseph Lyttle

Sources: The Greenwich Journal 17 Nov 1897; 18 Apr 1917; 29 Jun 1927; 3 May 1933; James Lyttle's Grandson William Almroth; Joseph Wever

James Wallace and The Linen Underwear Mill

Sources: The Greenwich Journal 10 Jun 1903

Chapter XIII - Some Memories Around Town

Memories of Ike Jackson

Sources: Ike Jackson

Memories of Two of Ireland's Own

Ivy Cooke Brown Cahill

Sources: Sara (Skiff) Idleman interview with Ivy

Jane Feenan Connor

Sources: Sara (Skiff) Idleman interview with Jane

Index of Terms in Volume 1

Batten Kill	Kill means stream in Dutch. The Hudson valley was first settled by the Dutch. New York was first known as New Holland. The Batten Kill flows into the Hudson and was named by those early settlers.
doubling	The process of taking one or more slivers of flax and combining them and then drawing them. This is done to produce an even sliver of flax.
drawing	The process of thinning out flax fibers. In manual spinning this is done by passing the flax through ones fingers as it enters the flyer. In automated processes this is done by two pairs of rollers.
dressed line	Flax that had been hackled.
doffer	One who takes the spools of thread off the spinning and roving machines (they do off).
flyer	On a spinning frame the flyer is what spins the fiber. The arms of the flyer also wind the spun thread onto the spool.
gill drawing	Gills in this case are fine needles used in the drawing process. The gills travel with the flax fiber between the pairs of rollers.
gill nets	Nets used in fishing which catches the fish by the gills. Linen thread was often used to make gill nets.
hackle	A device that looks like a small bed of nails. Each of the nails is about 3 inches long. It was used by a hackler to remove and remaining outer bark from the flax.
hank	A measure of thread.
lap	When the flax would take a trip around the rollers of a preparing or spinning machine it was called a lap.
noils	Very short fibers of flax used in making paper and very course threads.
plied thread	A thread consisting of several strands.
scutch	The process of removing the outer bark and inner core of flax straw.
reeler	One who reals the thread into hanks of fixed length.
ret	The process of rotting the gum which holds the flax fiber to the stalk of the flax straw.
ripple	The process of removing the leaves and seed pods from flax straw.
roughing	The process of combing the flax with a large wide tooth comb to ready the flax for hackling.
rove	Flax fiber which had a slight twist added to it. It would look like a thread but lacked significant strength.
tow	Short flax fibers. These fibers were used to make lower grade treads and twines.
wet spin	The process of spinning flax fibers after they have been passed through hot water.

Index to Volume 1

H. K., 38
Corvin
  James, 95
cottage industry, 109
Cotton, 22, 112, 147
  scarcity of, 104
cotton gin, 22
Cottrell
  Adam, 85, 87
  Betsey, 87
  Charles H., 85-87
  Estate of Charles H., 87
  Grace, 87
  Horton, 86, 87
  John, 87
  Martha, 87
  Mary, 86, 87
  Nathan, 87
  Susan, 87
  Terence, 87
  Walter, 87
Coumo
  Loretta, 11
County Armagh
  Bessbrook, 31
  Newry, 154
Courtney
  Rachel, 152
Couser, 34
  A., 57
  Andrew, 28
  Diana, 12
  Robert, 10
  Thomas, 28, 57, 134
  Thomas I., 39
  Walter J., 132
Cozzens
  Leonard, 38
Crandall, 57
  Mr. and Mrs. John, 60
Crawford Brothers, 112
cricket, 37
Cricket Club, 55
Crommelin
  Louis, 103
Crossen, 34
  Edward, 13, 28, 57
Crosson
  Edward, 54
Crothers
  Robert, 21
Crowe
  Mildred, 12
Crozier
  Jack, 32, 126
  John, 132
  Margaret (Neill), 136
  Richard, 125

Richard J., 132
Richard, Jr., 133
Sam, 99, 125
Samuel, 14, 20, 126, 136
Samuel, Jr., 13, 132
crushed fingers, 95
Cuba, 128
Cunningham
  Rev. R. J., 121
curfew, 84
Curry, 119
  Belle, 138
  Isabella, 10
  Mary, 138
Cutting Back - The Demand
  Declines, 50
cutting the Belfast Block, 125
Daisy
  G. D., 99
  George, 19, 20, 44, 47, 51,
    85, 92, 123, 129, 153,
    154
  Miss Ella, 61
  Mr. and Mrs. Arch, 61
dam, 41, 87, 146
  concrete, 83, 84
  lumber and stones, 83, 84
dancing, 141
Davidson
  Robert, 130
  William, 14
Davies
  J., 102
Davis
  Mrs., 60
Davison, 34
  James, 20
  William, 10, 28, 95
Day Care Center, 126
Dean
  Corbin, 38
Dean of Dunbarton Workmen,
  97
Death of Agnes Devine - the
  First Tragedy, 71
Debrick
  Eddington, 21
decorated
  gallantry in battle, 136
DeGregory
  Peg, 13
Delavergne
  Joseph, 128
DeLongo
  Theresa, 44
demand for shoe repairs, 50
Denaro
  Anthony, 130

Michael, 62, 130
depression, 64
DeRagan
  Kenneth, 73
Derby
  Peg, 12
Descent of Companies, 101
Devine, 34
  Agnes, 71
  baby, 71
  Elizabeth, 71
  James, 128
  John, 28, 71
  Lizza, 37
  William, 17, 28, 40, 60, 71
  William J., 37, 134
Dew retting, 3
Dewell
  John H., 46
Dickenson
  James, 104
Dickenson brothers, 106
Dickson
  James, 26
dig worms, 151
dissolved
  Barbour Flax Spinning
    Company, 102
  Dunbarton Flax Spinning
    Company, 102
  Finlayson Flax-Spinning
    Company, 112
  Linen Thread Company,
    114
  Marshall & Co., 112
Dittay
  Mr. and Mrs. William, 59
Doan
  John, 142
Doffers, 10, 152
Doffing, 94
Donnelly
  Sarah, 119
Doole
  Dorcas, 12
  Helen, 10
Dooley, 119
  Michael, 35, 65
Dornan
  Richard, 61
Doubleday
  Catherine, 13
  James, 16, 17, 99
  James E., 132
  Mr., 58
  Mr. and Mrs. Thomas, 59
  Norris, 133
  Robert, 119

flax storage, 75, 79
flax store house, 43, 81
flax tow, 43, 80
flax waste, 80
Flemming, 34
    Lizzie, 11
    Robert, 10
Fletcher
    Charlotte K., 11
    Ellen, 11
    John, 12
    Patrick E., 12, 132
    William J., 12, 130
flood plain, 40
Floods, 40
Florida
    Tampa, 128
florist business, 98
flume, 36, 41, 75, 82, 83, 146
Flute Bands, 58
flutes, 58
Flynn
    girls, 154
    Margaret, 13
    Thomas, 37
foreign flax, 22, 64
foreign money orders, 139
foreman, 99
forge, 146
forge house, 75
Forsythe
    Robert, 137
    Robert H., 18
Fort Wayne hospital, 128
Fourth of July, 81
France, 22, 24
    Argonne, 130
    Hams, 129
French Huguenots, 103
freshet, 84
Friday
    Shirley (Garrett, 17
    Shirley (Garrett), 125
Fullerton, 34
    John, Jr., 133
Fulmer
    Mr., 123
garage, 142
Garrett
    Shirley, 18
Garvey
    Mr. and Mrs. John, 59
Gatherwood
    John, 17
Geer
    Mr. and Mrs. John, 60
George Herrmann, Inc, vii
Georgia

Atlanta, 129
Getgood
    G., 57
Getwood, 34
Gibson
    Mr. E. H., 35
Giffen, 34
    John, 10, 137
Giffin
    Bella, 10, 12
    Jennie, 12
    John, 8, 121
    Mary, 10
Gilchrist
    Miss Grace, 61
Gilday, 34
Gilford House, 107
Gill
    J., 57
gilling twine, 63
Goodrich
    Blanche, 60
    Frank, 128
    Mr. and Mrs., 60
Gorham
    J. P., 60
Graduation from high school, 94
Graham
    N., 57
Gravlin
    Allen, 12
    Arthur M., 132
    Lillian, 46, 99
Gray
    Dr., 35
    Harry, 57
Great Britain, 114
great depression, 64
Greek revival, 126
Greenwich & Johnsonville Depot, 128
Greenwich & Johnsonville Railroad Depot, 132
Greenwich and Easton Elgin Butter and Cheese factory, 142
Greenwich and Johnsonville Railroad, 35, 40, 65
Greenwich before and after the Dunbarton, 124
Greenwich Chamber of Commerce, 52
Greenwich Cricket Club, 55
    field captain, 56
    President, 56
    secretary, 56
    treasurer, 56

    vice-president, 56
Greenwich Linen Company, 24, 40, 84, 85
Greenwich Linen Mill, 34
Griffin
    C. , 57
    Charles, 56
grist mill, 141
grocery store, 141
group photograph, 58
Gylday
    Catherine, 37
hackle bar, 148
hackle pins, 148
hackle shop, 40, 78
hackled flax, 90
hacklers, 93
Hackling, 4, 8, 78
Hall
    Maggie, 11
Hamel, 34
    Isabella, 13, 37
    James, 37
    Mary Ann, 37
    Robert, 37
    Sarah, 10, 13, 37
    Susan, 37
    William J., 17
Hamill
    James, 39
    Robert, 39
Hamilton Trust Co., 111
Hammel
    Robert, 121
Hammill
    Mr. and Mrs., 60
    Robert, 60
Hand
    Aaron A., 132
hanks, 148
Hanley
    Mrs. James, 61
Hanson Industries, Inc., 114
Hanson Trust Company, Ltd, 114
Hardigan
    Rev. R., 120
Harding
    Reverend J., 122
hardwood, 82
harp, 117
Harrington
    Raymond, 16
hate, 117
Haverley
    Cora M., 18
Hayes
    Fredrick W, 113

www.ingramcontent.com/pod-product-compliance
Lightning Source LLC
Chambersburg PA
CBHW070915270326
41927CB00011B/2586